eBAY

BUY AND SELL SUCCESSFULLY ON eBay.com

NICK VANDOME

BARNES & NOBLE BOOKS

NEW YORK

In easy steps is an imprint of Computer Step
Southfield Road · Southam
Warwickshire CV47 0FB · United Kingdom
www.ineasysteps.com

This edition published for Barnes & Noble Books, New York
FOR SALE IN THE USA ONLY
www.bn.com

Notice of Liability
Every effort has been made to ensure that this book contains accurate and
current information. However, Computer Step and the author shall not be
liable for any loss or damage suffered by readers as a result of any information
contained herein.

Trademarks
All trademarks are acknowledged as belonging to their respective companies.

Printed and bound in the United Kingdom

ISBN 0-7607-7488-9

Table of Contents

Beginning to buy 61

Bidding in an auction 73

Listing items for sale 91

Advanced listing   113

Conducting an auction   137

Feedback   147

Introducing eBay

eBay is an online marketplace, which has managed to become a multi-million dollar business while still retaining a genuine sense of being an online community where all of the members can influence the operation of the site. This chapter introduces the workings of eBay and shows how you can start using the world's largest online retail market.

Covers

Chapter One

History of eBay

Like all great inventions, simplicity is one of the foundations of eBay. It is not an online shop, as such, and it does not directly deal with goods or financial transactions. What it does do is enable buyers and sellers of a huge variety of products to do business with each other in a safe, friendly and efficient online environment. Essentially, eBay is the online middleman that facilitates the transactions without being involved in them directly.

eBay began in California in 1995 when Pierre Omidyar hit on a simple but brilliant idea for an online business: to create a trading environment where buyers and sellers could meet to sell products. eBay was launched in September 1995, at the height of the dotcom boom. Initially the site was not intended to create a huge user base but it soon started attracting more and more people. Originally, Pierre had wanted to call it Echo Bay, but as that name was already taken by another business it had to be shortened to the now familiar global brand, eBay.

There are various stories relating to the first item that was sold on eBay: one says it was a broken laser pointer, while the other claims it was a Pez dispenser for peppermint sweets. The official version on the eBay site goes with the Pez option.

eBay has five basic values by which the site operates. These can be accessed in full from the Community pages within eBay.

The growth of eBay has been astonishing: not only has it survived the dotcom crash and seen off the inevitable imitators, but it has expanded to the point where it has over 100 million registered users and sites in over 20 countries around the world. What at one time was dismissed as an online gimmick has now become a global force in the world of commerce.

The original idea of eBay was that it would be for individuals to sell items through auctions: the item would be placed on the site and the highest bid would secure it. This is still the essence of eBay, although two important developments have taken place since the site was first launched. Firstly, individuals and mainstream retailers have realized the potential of eBay and set up full-time businesses through the website. Secondly, more and more high-priced items, such as cars and, in some countries, houses and real estate, are now available on the site.

Some of the more unusual items put up for sale on eBay include a 50,000-year-old mammoth skeleton, Britney Spears' used bubble gum and a Vulcan Bomber.

Although there are strict rules about what can be sold on eBay, almost anything can be put up for auction as long as it meets these rules. If you are looking to buy and sell products in a wide variety of categories then you cannot afford to ignore eBay: it is a huge global marketplace, it is largely self-regulating and it is great fun. If you have never entered the world of eBay, now is the time.

What you can do on eBay

Although eBay is constantly evolving and developing, the essence of the site is still the same: a seller posts an item for auction, people bid for it, and the highest bidder purchases the item. While buying and selling remains the cornerstone of the eBay community, there is a lot more that can be done:

Children under the age of 18 are not allowed to register as members on eBay, but they are permitted to use the site under the supervision of an adult.

Browse

You can browse through the massive eBay database of items currently for sale. This is not only enlightening as far as the range of items available is concerned, but it is also an invaluable way for sellers to see if there are similar items to theirs for sale.

View auctions

It is perfectly possible and allowable to view auctions that are currently taking place, without having to place a bid. This gives you a good idea of how the process works and can be a good indicator of the perceived value of certain items.

For more information on the Buy It Now option, see Chapter Four.

Buy It Now

If you do not want to participate in an auction, it is still possible to buy some items at a single click, with the Buy It Now button. This is an option that allows sellers to enter the product at a fixed price as well as, or instead of, the auction.

Feedback

Feedback is vital to the smooth running of the eBay community, and both buyers and sellers are actively encouraged to leave feedback whenever they have been involved in any sort of transaction. Once you have bought or sold a few items you will come to realize the importance of feedback.

For more information on Feedback, see Chapter Nine.

Customize

How you use eBay can be customized using the My eBay page that is available to every registered user. This enables you to perform a variety of auction-related tasks in one location.

For more information on the My eBay page, see Chapter Three.

Communicate

A vital part of any auction is the facility to ask the seller questions about the product they are selling. In addition, there is also a vibrant eBay online community where all issues relating to eBay, and other topics, can be discussed.

First view

When the eBay site is first accessed the opening screen is, in effect, an introduction to eBay and, while some of the functions can be accessed, you have to register before you can start buying and selling items.

To view the initial eBay home page, enter www.ebay.com into your browser:

1 Click here to access the main areas of eBay

2 Click here to find out more about buying and selling on eBay

In some previous versions of eBay, and for some global sites, the initial page looks slightly different depending on whether you have registered.

3 Click one of the options on the main navigation bar to move to that page

home | pay | register | services | site map

| Buy | Sell | My eBay | Community | Help |

4 Certain areas within eBay can be viewed even if you have not registered. Here, you can see the categories of goods that are for sale

Getting registered

You can view items for sale without having to register on eBay. However, if you want to place a bid, or find out more information about an auction, the seller or other bidders, you have to go through the registration process.

If you want to do anything more on eBay than have a general look around then you have to become a registered user. This is free, and once you are registered it means that you can start buying and selling items on eBay. Since eBay takes issues of security and personal information very seriously, you will, in most cases, have to enter credit card details to confirm that the name and address you have given are correct. To register on eBay:

1 Click here on the home page

or

Click here on the main toolbar

2 Enter your personal details, such as your name, address and telephone number

3 Continue by entering an email address

Important: A valid email address is required to complete registration.

Email address
nickvandome@hotmail.com
Examples: myname@yahoo.com, myname@example.com, etc.

Re-enter email address
nickvandome@hotmail.com

Your User ID is the name by which you will be identified whenever you bid, buy or sell anything on eBay. It is possible to change your User ID once you have created it.

4 Check this box on to accept the User Agreement

eBay User Agreement and Privacy Policy (Printer-friendly version)

eBay User Agreement and Privacy Policy
User Agreement

THE FOLLOWING DESCRIBES THE TERMS ON WHICH EBAY OFFERS YOU ACCESS TO OUR SERVICES.

Welcome to the user agreement (the "Agreement" or "User Agreement") for eBay Inc. If you reside outside of the United States, the party you are

Please check the box below:
☑ I agree to the following:
 • I accept the User Agreement and Privacy Policy above.
 • I may receive communications from eBay and I understand that I can change my notification preferences at any time in My eBay.

5 Click Continue

[Continue >]

6 If you have entered any incorrect details, or missed out any that are required by eBay, the same page will appear but with the outstanding fields highlighted in red

Do not enter incorrect contact information when registering. If you do, the details will probably be different from those held on your credit card and you will not be able to complete the registration process.

ebaY

Register: Enter Information   Help

① **Enter Information**   2. Choose User ID & Password   3. Check Your Email

⚠ The following must be corrected before continuing:
 • First name - Please enter this information.
 • Last name - - Please enter this information.
 • Zip Code - Your zip/postal code must be numeric.
 • Address - Please enter this information.
 • Primary telephone - Phone Number is Invalid.
 • Date of Birth - Your Date of Birth is invalid.

Register now to bid or buy on **any** eBay site. It's easy and **free!**

⚠ Please enter this information.   ⚠ Please enter this information.
First name   **Last name**
[   ]   [   ]

⚠ Please enter this information.
Street address
[   ]

7 Complete the required fields and resend the form

8 Enter a User ID, password and reminder question

Register: Choose User ID & Password   Help

1. Enter Information   2 **Choose User ID & Password**   3. Check Your Email

Choose an eBay User ID
Your User ID identifies you to other eBay users.
- nickv7867
- 7867nickv
- vandome7867
- Create your own ID: [   ]

Create password
[   ]
6 character minimum.
Enter a password that's easy for you to remember, but hard for others to guess. See tips.

How secure is your password?
[   ]
The meter above suggests how secure your password might be. If your password scores all 3 bars, it is relatively secure.

Re-enter password
[   ]

If you forget your User ID, or your password, you can contact eBay from a link on the Sign In page and have it sent to your email address.

9 Click Continue

Secret question
[What is your mother's maiden name? ▾]

Secret answer
[Mother]

You will be asked for the answer to your secret question if you forget your password.

[Continue >]

10 You need to confirm your identity by entering your credit card details. This is to ensure that the details you have given during registration match those

eBay has very strict privacy policies to ensure that credit details are only used for verifying your identity. These details will not be divulged to a third party.

Register: Confirm Identity   Help

1. Enter Information   2 **Choose User ID & Password**   3. Check Your Email

Registration is **free** . However, we require a credit or debit card to confirm your identity. This helps keep eBay a safe place to buy and sell.

👁 Live help - Chat online with a Customer Support representative.

Your card will **not** be charged or shared with eBay sellers. Your personal information is protected by eBay's Privacy Policy and encrypted by industry-standard software.

Credit or debit card number
[   ]
Visa, Mastercard, American Express, or Discover

Expiration date
[–Month– ▾] [–Year– ▾]

Cardholder information (change)
Nick Vandome
Main Street
Boston, Massachusetts 01720
United States

[Continue >]

associated with your credit card. Once this has been confirmed, click the Continue button to finalize your registration

Categories

Category placement is up to the seller and depends on the selection that they make when they register an item for auction.

The main objective for most people who visit eBay is to buy or sell items. In both cases it is important to know what you are looking for and where to find it: buyers will want to locate the items they want to purchase and sellers may want to research similar items that are already on sale and see where they have been placed on eBay. One of the ways to look for items on eBay is to browse through the Categories lists. These can be accessed from the home page and then sub-categories can be located. In some instances, several levels have to be navigated until you find the item you are looking for, but it is a useful way to become familiar with the categories of items that are available on eBay. To look for an item using Categories:

Because of the fluid nature of eBay, the Categories headings do change from time to time, to accommodate changing trends.

1 Click one of the main categories on the home page

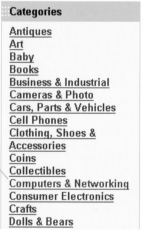

Categories

Antiques
Art
Baby
Books
Business & Industrial
Cameras & Photo
Cars, Parts & Vehicles
Cell Phones
Clothing, Shoes & Accessories
Coins
Collectibles
Computers & Networking
Consumer Electronics
Crafts
Dolls & Bears

Browsing through the Categories is a good way to get an idea of the types of items available on eBay. However, after a while you may find that a more efficient way of finding items is to use the eBay search facility.

2 Click one of the sub-categories to drill down further through the list

COMPUTERS & NETWORKING

	Computers & Networking

Categories within Computers & Networking

Apple, Macintosh Computers
Apple Components
Apple Desktops
Apple Drives, Media
Apple Input Devices
Apple Laptops, Notebooks
Apple Monitors/Displays
Apple Networking
Apple Parts & Accessories
Printers, Scanners & Ink
Vintage Apple/Macintosh
Other Apple Products
Wholesale Lots

Desktop PC Components
Cables, Adapter Cards
CPUs for Desktop PC
Fans, Heatsinks, Cooling
Memory for Desktop PC

Laptop Parts & Accessories
Adapters, Chargers for Laptops
Batteries for Laptops
Cables, Connectors for Laptops
Cases, Bags for Laptops
CPUs for Laptops
Docking Stations for Laptops
Drives for Laptops
Keyboards for Laptops
Memory Upgrades for Laptops
Mice, Mouse for Laptops
Motherboards for Laptops
PCMCIA Cards for Laptops
Repair, Service Manuals
Screens, LCD Panel for Laptops
Security for Laptops
Video & Sound for Laptops
Other Parts & Accessories
Wholesale Lots

3 A display page shows the current items being auctioned in the selected category

By default, search results pages show the relevant items sorted by the least time left in the current auctions, so that the auctions that are nearest to ending are listed first. This can be changed by clicking on the arrows in the Sort By box and selecting a different option.

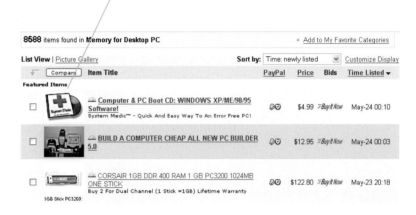

4 To refine the search within the selected category, or sub-category, enter a keyword into the Search box at the top of the page

5 The search page now displays the results determined by the search keyword criteria

Searching for items

Instead of drilling down through the Categories, another way to look for items is to use the eBay search engine. This operates in a similar way to an Internet search engine (such as Google) and, if used accurately, it can be an excellent way of locating specific items. To use the Search facility:

Keyword searches look at the titles and descriptions that have been given to an item by the seller.

1 The search box is located on the main eBay navigation bar

If you are having difficulty finding something through the use of keywords, try using alternate spellings, or even misspellings, of the keywords.

2 Enter a keyword here for the item you want to locate, and click the Search button

3 The results page shows the number of matches that have been found and lists them according to the properties that were set in the initial search. It is then possible to view a particular item by clicking on its link

Once you have accessed an item from the Search results page you can then participate in the auction by placing a bid. However, you have to be a registered user before you can do this.

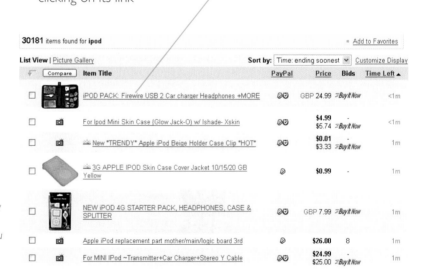

Refining a search

If too many results are returned from an initial search keyword then you may want to refine the search to limit the results to just the items you want. This can be done by entering additional search criteria:

If you want to find an item with an exact phrase, include it within inverted commas, e.g. "Barbie doll outfits". This will ensure a more accurate search. If you want to search for an item with one specific attribute, enter a plus sign before the attribute.

1. Enter additional words or phrases in the Search box. In this case the minus sign (-) indicates that we do not want any items with the word "mini" in the results

> ipod -mini
>
> ☐ Search title **and** description

If you want to broaden a search, tick the Search Title and Description box underneath the main search box. This will then search over the description of the item that the seller has provided rather than just the main title. This can result in a significantly greater number of search results.

2. The search results reflect the amended search criteria and only include the items as specified in the search

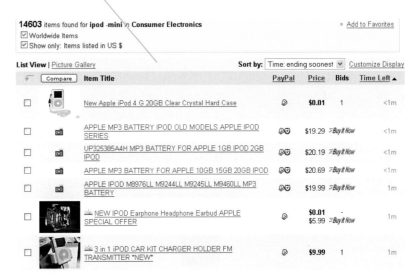

3 To further refine
the search criteria
when looking for

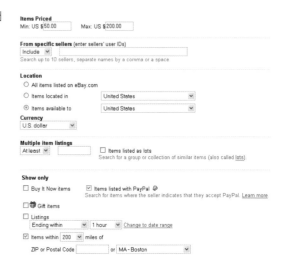

items, click here next to the Search button

4 Enter the required
details to refine
your search.
This can include
information such
as price, location,
currency and
the condition
of goods. Click
Search to see the
results

*As you become
more experienced
at searching for
items on eBay
you may find
that you only need to enter the
correct keywords and details in
the search box. However, the
More Search Options box can be
useful for specific occasions, such
as where you want to limit the
results by price.*

5 The search results are narrowed down even further

Creating favorite searches

If there are certain items that you want to look for on a regular basis, it is possible to save a search for a particular item and then access it whenever you want, to see how the results for that item have changed over time. To create a Favorite search:

1 Click here at the top of the results page once a search has been completed

You can create dozens of Favorite Searches; this is a good way of keeping track of what is becoming available for a variety of items.

2 Select the details for how you want the Favorite search to operate and click the Save Search button

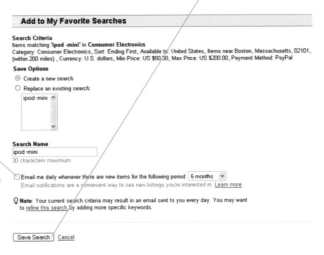

If you tick this box and specify a time frame, you will be sent an email whenever anything new comes up for auction within these search criteria.

3 On the Search page a list of Favorite Searches appears as a drop-down list and can be accessed by clicking the Go button. The results will be displayed for the items at any given time, since they change depending on which auctions are taking place

Stores

Due to its remarkable level of success, eBay has become more than just a location for individuals to buy and sell their old record collections or antique teddy bears. There are now a number of speciality sites that are, in effect, online stores. They are run mainly by online retailers rather than individuals, and, although a lot of them conduct auctions for their goods, a large number of items are sold at a set price. The eBay Stores can be accessed from the Speciality Sites box on the home page:

As the popularity of eBay increases, more and more retailers are realizing the benefit of having an online presence. This has resulted in a greater number of eBay stores.

1 Click here to see the range of online stores (this tends to change fairly regularly as online retailers, just like the bricks and mortar ones, come and go)

Some eBay stores display only Buy It Now items, which means you can only buy them at the price displayed, in the same way as a conventional retailer. Other stores have an auction option as well as Buy It Now. For more information on Buy It Now see Chapter Four.

2 The range of stores is displayed here

3 Click on a logo to see the goods for that store

4 Items can be bid on or bought at a set price in the same way as eBay auctions between individuals

Motors

eBay has a special category for shops that are used exclusively to sell cars and related accessories. Since this invariably involves larger sums than a lot of other eBay auctions, a certain amount of caution is required when dealing with this type of transaction. Treat it in the same way as buying a car from a classified advertisement, and if possible go to see the vehicle before you bid for it. Also, have a very careful look at the description of the vehicle and the payment and delivery details. To use the Motors shop, access it from the eBay Motors link on the home page.

Because of the large sums of money that can be involved, it is vital that you find out as much as possible about the vehicle in which you are interested and also the person selling it. If you are involved in transactions with large sums of money, there are ways to try and ensure the money is held safely until the deal has been done. This is known as escrow and is looked at in detail in Chapter Ten.

1 Enter a vehicle type here to search for a particular model of car, or…

2 Click on a link to see the models for that category

3 The results are displayed in the same way as for any other auction. Click on a link to see details of a particular listed car

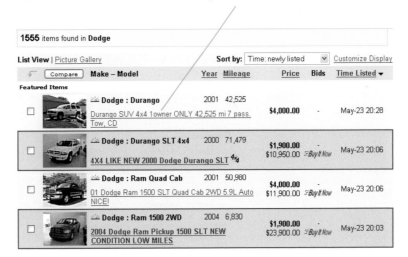

4 The description and auction details are the same as for any other item. Bids can be made by clicking on the Place Bid button

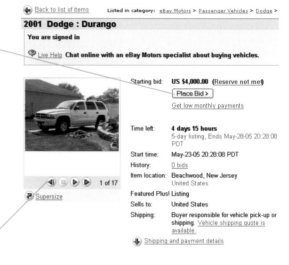

Back to list of items Listed in category: eBay Motors > Passenger Vehicles > Dodge >

2001 Dodge : Durango

You are signed in

Live Help **Chat online with an eBay Motors specialist about buying vehicles.**

Starting bid: **US $4,000.00** (Reserve not met)

Place Bid >

Get low monthly payments

Time left: **4 days 15 hours**
5-day listing, Ends May-28-05 20:28:08 PDT

Start time: May-23-05 20:28:08 PDT

History: 0 bids

Item location: Beachwood, New Jersey, United States

Featured Plus! Listing

Sells to: **United States**

Shipping: Buyer responsible for vehicle pick-up or shipping. Vehicle shipping quote is available.

Shipping and payment details

1 of 17

Supersize

If you are not happy with the photographs that are displayed for a particular vehicle, or, even worse, there are no pictures, then do not proceed with bidding on the auction.

5 Click here to view additional pictures of the vehicle

6 Click on a thumbnail image to see larger pictures of the vehicle

Enlarge this picture

Select a picture

When entering into an auction on the Motors site, email the seller, to ask them specific questions and also to get a general feel for how they conduct business.

7 Scroll down the page to see a full description of the vehicle

Description

Item Specifics - Automobiles
Dodge : Durango
Durango SUV 4x4 1owner ONLY 42,525 mi 7 pass. Tow, CD

Miles:	**42525**
Transmission:	**Automatic**
Warranty:	Free 1 month/1,000 mile Service Agreement
Title:	**Clear**
Condition:	**Used**
Engine:	**8 CYLINDER 4.7 LITER**

Doors:	**4 doors**
Interior:	**Gray**
Year:	**2001**
VIN Number:	1b4hs28n31f598721
	Get the Vehicle History Report
Exterior:	**White**
Inspection:	--

Want It Now

As well as facilities for people selling things, eBay has an option where you can tell people what you are looking for, in the hope that you can match up with someone who has a similar item to sell. This streamlines the buying and selling process as it removes the need for an auction. This option is known as Want It Now. To use it:

1　Click here under Speciality Sites

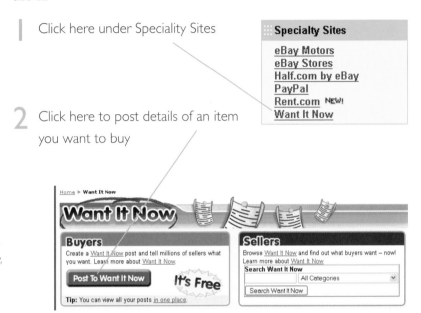

2　Click here to post details of an item you want to buy

Once items have been placed on the Want It Now page, sellers can view the items or search for specific items. This way, buyers and sellers can match up their requirements.

3　Enter a description of the desired item and click here. The details will then be posted on a Want It Now board which anyone can view. If someone has a similar item to the one in which you are interested they will contact you to conduct a sale

Selling on Want It Now

Want It Now can also be used by sellers to find people who are looking for items that they are looking to sell. To do this:

1 Enter the details here of the item you have to sell

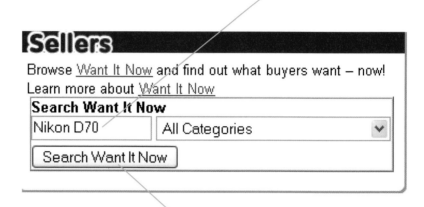

2 Click the Search Want It Now button

3 The matching items that people are looking for are listed here

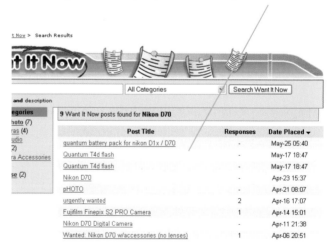

4 Click on an item to view further details about it

5 View the details of the item for which someone is looking

Placed in category: Cameras & Photo

| Quantum T4d flash | | Post number: 7517103251 |

| Responses: | 0 total responses | Time left: | **45 days 15 hours** | **Buyer information** |

Respond >

Date placed: May-17-05 18:47:40 PDT

Location: Broomall , PA United States

Feedback Score: 10
Positive Feedback: **100%**
Member since Sep-02-00 in United States

Description

Flash for nikon D70

6 Click the Respond button if you have an item to sell that matches the one listed on Want It Now

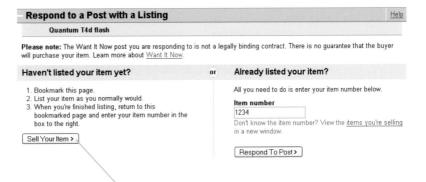

Respond to a Post with a Listing   Help

Quantum T4d flash

Please note: The Want It Now post you are responding to is not a legally binding contract. There is no guarantee that the buyer will purchase your item. Learn more about Want It Now.

Haven't listed your item yet?   or   **Already listed your item?**

1. Bookmark this page.
2. List your item as you normally would.
3. When you're finished listing, return to this bookmarked page and enter your item number in the box to the right.

Sell Your Item >

All you need to do is enter your item number below.

Item number

1234

Don't know the item number? View the items you're selling in a new window.

Respond To Post >

7 Click the Sell Your Item button if you have not already listed the item for sale, or click the Respond To Post button if you have already listed the item and you want to direct the person to the existing listing. Then the person looking for the item can either participate in an auction or use the Buy It Now option, if it is available

Half.com

Linked from eBay is a site called Half.com. This is an online shop that offers items such as CDs, video games, software programs and computer hardware. It operates in the same way as any online shop and the prices are fixed by the sellers, who are usually individuals or small businesses. To use Half.com

1 Click here under Speciality Sites

2 You can log in to Half.com using your eBay User ID and Password

3 Click here to browse the categories on Half.com and start shopping. Items can be bought in the same way as on any other online retail site

Rent.com

Another speciality site that can be accessed through eBay is Rent.com. This is a site that provides information about rental accommodation and enable people who are looking for accommodation to get in touch with the people who are renting it. To use Rent.com

Click here under Speciality Sites

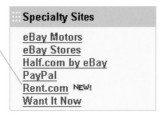

When renting accommodation through Rent. com, make the same rigorous checks as you would for rented accommodation through any other form of advertising.

Enter the details about the type of accommodation in which you are interested

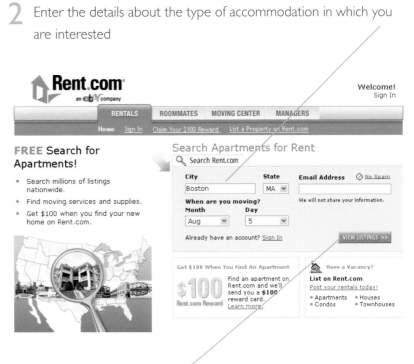

Click the View Listings button to see matching accommodation. You have to register on Rent.com to use this service, but registration is free and only requires minimal details

Charity auctions

Charities are constantly trying to find new ways of generating revenue. eBay has a dedicated site on which charities can promote their causes and sell items to raise funds. These items have often been donated by celebrities and they are frequently signed.

Charities register on eBay to sell items in the same way as anyone else and they have to pay the same fees. However, their auctions receive free promotion and they can create an About Me page to give additional information about the charity.

To view charity auctions, click here on the home page

Business Marketplace
eBay Pulse
Giving Works (Charity)
Live Auctions
Solutions Directory
Wholesale

One of the most questionable categories of item that are sold on eBay is celebrity autographs. There are a lot of these for sale in charity auctions but in general these are more authentic than for standard eBay auctions. Always be careful about autographed items that are not charity auctions.

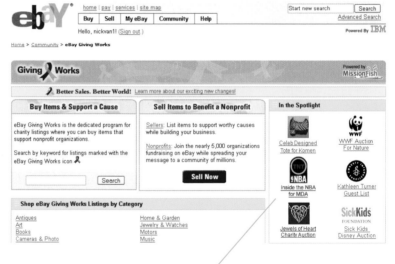

Click here to view current charity auctions or select a charity from the category listings

Communities

One of the founding philosophies of eBay is that it should be a community of users who communicated and interacted with one another rather than just processing commercial transactions. Despite its huge financial success, this ethos has remained on eBay and the concept of a huge online community is as strong as ever. In recognition of this, there is an individual site devoted to the eBay community. This includes discussion boards, news and announcements, upcoming events and general community values. To participate in the eBay community:

The Community area also contains the latest news and announcements from eBay. These cover a variety of topics and reading them is a good way to keep up with the latest developments.

1 Click here on the main navigation bar

eBay staff members participate in discussion boards and chatboards and this can be an invaluable source of information regarding the site.

2 Click on one of the links to go to that page within the community. Some areas, such as the discussion boards, have a huge amount of information and comments within them

3 Within an area such as the discussion boards it is possible to find out more general information about them, view what is being said by others and also add your own comments

It is perfectly allowable to view the postings on the discussion boards without posting anything yourself. This is known as "lurking" but it is not generally frowned upon.

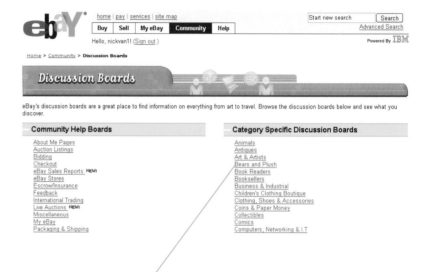

4 Click on a link to view a specific discussion board

5 The individual conversation threads are displayed and can be followed by clicking on the links

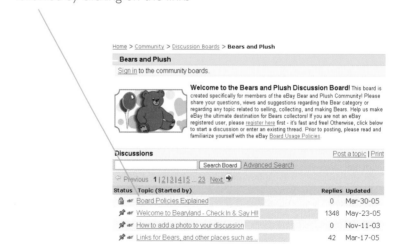

International eBays

eBay is a global phenomenon with sites in over 20 countries around the world. However, in keeping with the community nature of eBay, it is possible to buy and sell items on any of these sites, as long as the seller is prepared to send the items internationally. Once you have registered, or logged in, you can operate on any eBay site in the same way as you would on the one in your own country. To view eBay sites around the world:

1. Enter a country name in the Global Sites search box on the home page

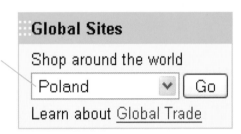

2. Some international sites have a familiar look and feel and they can be used in the same way as any other eBay site

European eBay sites look very similar to the US version. Some sites, such as those in Latin America and Asia, have their own individual characteristics and appearances.

3 It is possible to log in to international sites and view areas such as My eBay as you would with your local site. You can also buy and sell items on these sites, but the

seller will have to be prepared to ship items internationally

On some international sites, there are translations for the items on sale. However, unless you have a good grasp of the language of the site, think twice before you enter into an auction as the translations are not guaranteed.

4 Some international sites are designed specifically for the region in which they appear, while others are existing auction sites that have been taken over by eBay

If you are going to bid for items on international sites, make sure that the sellers are prepared to post the items to the country in which you live and not just their own. It is important to do this before you bid rather than afterwards.

5 When conducting searches, if there are no items in your own locality then there will be a listing for other locations in which similar items are for sale

Live auctions

Although eBay auctions can be exciting, particularly towards the end of them, they cannot match live auctions in an auction house. This is addressed by eBay by providing a service where you can view live auctions as they happen around the world. Although this is accessed from the US version of eBay, it can be viewed by users anywhere in the world and, if you sign up, you can bid for the items that are available on the live auction site. To access live auctions:

To bid in Live Auctions, you have to go through a separate login process to the standard one for logging in to eBay.

1 View the eBay site at www.ebay.com and click on the Live Auctions link under Categories

2 Click here to view a live auction in progress. Since they happen in real-time, the action is very fast-paced

Live auctions can contain some very high-priced items and they move very quickly. Unless you are very sure that you want to participate, it can be better to view these auctions rather than join in with them.

3 The bids in the live auction are displayed here, as they happen

4 Click here to sign up to participate in live auctions and bid on items that appear on the live auction page

Finding help

eBay believes in helping users as much as possible and there is a site designed specifically for this. The pages cover all areas of eBay, from buying and selling to what happens when somebody does not pay for items they have won in an auction. To use the help pages:

1 Click here on the main navigation bar

The eBay Security Center offers a range of advice about buying and selling safely on eBay. There is a link to the Security Center at the bottom of most eBay pages.

2 Select a help topic from the list

Help Topics

Top Questions about eBay

1. What if my item sold and the winner didn't pay for it?
2. How can I end my listing immediately?
3. What steps can I take to trade safely on eBay?
4. Can I retract or cancel my bid?
5. How much does it cost to sell on eBay?

New to eBay
Registration | How to buy
How to sell | more...

Finding What You Are Looking For
Finding an Item | Finding Seller's other Items
Finding Members | more...

Buying
Buying Basics | Trusting the Seller
Finding an Item | more...

Using My eBay
Watching or Buying an Item | Preferences
My Account | more...

Account Information & Billing
My Personal Information | My Seller's Account
My About Me Page | more...

Rules and Policies
User Agreement | Privacy Policy
Prohibited and Restricted Items | more...

3 Most topics have links to additional information

Buying: Getting Started Overview

If you're new to buying on eBay, welcome! Thousands of items, from the practical to the peculiar, are waiting for you.

It's easy to learn what you need to know to make your first purchase.

- Take a guided tour of the buying process to get oriented.
- If you haven't already, you'll need to register as an eBay member. It's easy and free!
- Go through the buyer's checklist to make sure you're ready to buy.
- Ask questions, learn about buying and meet other eBay members in community boards and chat.
- Learn about My eBay, a valuable tool you'll want to use from your first bid to beyond your hundredth purchase.

Rules and regulations

The success of eBay is based on the users playing fair and ensuring that the integrity of the site is maintained. In order to support this there is a comprehensive list of rules and regulations that should be followed by eBay members. These also contain sanctions for when the rules are broken. This chapter looks at the various areas covered by the eBay rules, regulations and policies, and gives an overview of what should, and what should not, be done on the site.

Covers

Chapter Two

General

Given that eBay is a multi-million dollar industry it is perhaps surprising that it does not have more problems with fraud and unscrupulous behavior, particularly as most transactions take place online, between people who have never met, and who, in most cases, have never been in contact with each other. However, that is not to say that problems do not occur: they do. But with a bit of groundwork and preparation the careful eBayer can try and minimize the risk of infringing the rules or falling prey to a dishonest buyer or seller.

One of the five founding principles of eBay is that basically people are good. This is supported by the fact that the site has expanded so rapidly and so successfully in such a short period of time. But, as with anything involving money, problems do occur; some of the most common ones are:

As far as the legality of transactions on eBay is concerned, individuals are subject to the law of the country of the site on which they are conducting business.

- Problems with listings. People, either deliberately or accidentally, give a misleading or fraudulent description.

- Selling dubious items. eBay has an extensive list of prohibited, questionable and infringing items. While a lot of these get filtered out at the time of listing, some of them get through the net. If you are in any way unsure about whether an item should be on eBay or not, do not attempt to buy or sell it.

When buying items the best way to guard against fraud is to check the seller's feedback rating and then email them about the product, asking as many questions as you like. If in doubt, do not proceed.

- Sellers not sending the item as it is described. Sometimes sellers advertise items that are nothing like the product which the winning bidder receives. In some case this is due to laziness or simple inaccuracy, but in others it can be because of fraud. Due to the robust feedback system, fraudulent sellers usually do not last too long, but this is of little comfort if you have already fallen prey to one of them.

- Buyers not sending any payment. There are a number of reasons for this, but the golden rule is that you should never send an item until you have received payment for it. If the payment is by check, wait until it has cleared before you send the item. While non-payment can be annoying, it is still possible to re-list an item which has not been paid for.

Prohibited items

When you look at the list of categories of items for sale on eBay you may think that it is implausible for any items to be prohibited, but this is far from the case. eBay take matters of the law very seriously and there is an extensive list of items that are banned; this list is non-negotiable, and if you try to list one of these items then you will be subject to eBay's own sanctions and you may even face prosecution. Some of the prohibited items include credit cards, firearms, lock-picking devices, human parts and remains, lottery tickets, prescription drugs and any stolen items. A full list of prohibited items can be viewed on the eBay Policies page, which can be accessed from the link at the bottom of most eBay pages. For each prohibited item there is a link that contains an explanation of why that item is prohibited and, in some cases, exceptions to the general rule.

There is a large number of eBay staff who check listings, but some prohibited items do occasionally slip through.

Hazardous Materials

Hazardous or dangerous goods (such as explosives, radioactive materials, flammable gases, liquids and solids, and toxic substances) may pose a danger to health, safety or property while being transported, Many hazardous goods cannot be shipped through the mail or commercial carrier at all. Such items are not permitted on eBay. Please review the examples and additional information sections below for more information on specific limits and exceptions to this policy.

A few hazardous materials may legally be transported under certain conditions if they are properly packaged and labeled. Such items are permitted on eBay, provided that the listing contains a clear notice of the hazardous nature of the material, and a description of the planned method of shipping that complies with the law. For details on particular hazardous substances and transportation requirements in the US and internationally, look at the <u>U.S. Postal Service Publication 52</u>.

Violations of this policy may result in a range of actions, including:

If you enter a search keyword for a prohibited item, you may find a number of results. These will probably be related items, such as a book about a prohibited item, rather than the prohibited item itself.

Since each eBay site is subject to the law of its host country, there may be slight differences between their lists of prohibited items. For instance, the list for the US may be different to that for other countries due to legal and political considerations. Before you start selling on eBay, have a good look at the list of prohibited items: if you do transgress them then ignorance is not an excuse. Similarly, when purchasing items, if you think they may be prohibited, contact eBay to tell them about it and ask them for advice about how you should proceed. (See page 42 for details of how to do this.)

Questionable and infringing items

As well as prohibited items, there are equally extensive lists for questionable and infringing items, both of which should be read in full before you start selling.

Questionable items are regarded as those that can be sold only under certain circumstances. In some cases, each item of this type is judged on its merits. One of the questionable items is Adult Material, which is a good example of how the interpretation is not always clear-cut. The default position is that eBay does not allow the listing of erotica or sexually orientated material. However, if this type of material is included as part of another item then it may be allowed, as long as it is a small part and the main item does not fall into this category. Similarly, some artwork could be listed depending on the context.

Some software programs appear for sale with a description stating that they should only be used as backups if you have bought the original program. This is definitely a gray area and buyers should treat it with caution.

Infringing items are those that could infringe an existing copyright or trademark. The most common examples of this occur with software programs, video games and films. For instance, it is permissible to list a genuine, unused version of a software program, but unauthorized copies cannot be listed. The same applies for pirated video games and films. This is one area where it is relatively easy for unscrupulous sellers to pass off their goods as genuine when in fact they are copies. A quick search on eBay for any popular software program will bring up a number of results that are probably not genuine versions.

As with prohibited items, questionable and infringing items are subject to the law of the country in which the site is located. This can create some interesting regional issues. For example, on eBay.co.uk consider the sale of British Titles (which comes under the Questionable category). It is not permissible to sell or buy titles such as Duke and Duchess, Earl and Countess or Viscount and Viscountess, but it is allowable to list Scottish Feudal Baronies as long as it is stated that they are for Scotland and they are clearly and accurately described (these are available for all eBayers).

Because of the size of the site it is impossible for eBay to police every single auction. However, if you do get caught repeatedly breaking the rules you will probably be given three warnings and after that you will have your account suspended. This means that you will not be able to trade on the site until the suspension is lifted.

Listing policies

One of the ways in which eBay tries to enforce its policy on prohibited, questionable and infringing items is through its listing policies. These form an extensive list; some of the areas covered are:

Selling duplicate items within the same auction is known as a Dutch auction and this is looked at in more detail in Chapter Four.

- How to make sure that you list your product so that it appears in the correct category.

- How to list items if you are selling duplicate items within the same auction.

- Creating listings where you are offering a prize or free gift for the person who wins the final auction.

- The types of listing that are not permitted, such as those promoting prize competitions or lotteries, those which try to avoid paying the standard eBay fees, and those which include language that is abusive in terms of being racist, hateful, sexual or obscene.

- The eBay links policy. The details the types of links that can be used within a listing (usually to other areas within eBay) and those which cannot be used.

Full details of the listing policies can be found by following the Listing Policies link on the Policies page:

Click on a link to see details of a particular item within the Listing Policies

Listing Policies:

- About Me Guidelines
- Bonuses and Prizes
- Catalog Sales
- Categorization
- Cell Phone Service Contracts
- Choice Listings
- Circumventing Fees
- Duplicate Listings
- Excessive Shipping/Handling
- Giveaways, Raffles, and Prizes
- HTML and JavaScript
- Key Word Spamming
- Links
- Links Frequently Asked Questions
- Linking to Descriptions
- Linking from Your Email Address
- Linking to Photos
- Linking to About Me

User Agreement

Most people who have used computers will have come across User Agreements before, either when installing software or when purchasing items from an online retailer. In many cases, people simply click the Accept button when faced with these types of agreements and then move on to something more interesting. However, in the case of eBay and its User Agreement it is a good idea to read it in full. This is so that you understand what is expected of you while you are on the site and how you can expect others to behave towards you too. Also, the User Agreement contains a lot of useful general information about eBay, and it is a good introduction to the Do's and Don'ts of the site. To access the User Agreement:

1   Access the Policies page and click on the User Agreement link

2   If you have not already done so, take the time to read the User Agreement in full

Your User Agreement

User Agreement

THE FOLLOWING DESCRIBES THE TERMS ON WHICH EBAY OFFERS YOU ACCESS TO OUR SERVICES.

Welcome to the user agreement (the "Agreement" or "User Agreement") for eBay Inc. If you reside outside of the United States, the party you are contracting with is eBay International AG. This Agreement describes the terms and conditions applicable to your use of our services available under the domain and sub-domains of www.ebay.com (the "Site") (including half.ebay.com, stores.ebay.com) and the general principles for the websites of our subsidiaries and international affiliates. If you do not agree to be bound by the terms and conditions of this Agreement, do not use or access our services.

If you have any questions, please refer to our User Agreement Frequently Asked Questions or our User Agreement Revision Frequently Asked Questions.

Privacy

Another issue which is taken very seriously on eBay is privacy. Due to the amount of personal information that a member has to give before they can register on eBay (name, address, telephone number, email address and credit card details), it is imperative that this information is kept strictly for those people who require it and no-one else.

The privacy policy contains details of the type of information collected by eBay, what is done with it, who it is disclosed to and how you can change your personal details. To review the Privacy Policy:

1 Access the Help page and click on the Privacy Policy link

2 Click on a link to view that item in the policy, or scroll down to read the whole policy

Table of Contents

1. An Important Note About Children
2. Information We Collect
3. Our Use of Your Information
4. Our Disclosure of Your Information
    ◇ Advertisers
    ◇ eBay Community
    ◇ External Service Providers
    ◇ Internal Service Providers for Our Operations
    ◇ Other Corporate Entities
    ◇ Legal Requests
5. Your Use of Other Users' Information
6. Use of Email Tools
7. Control of Your Password
8. Accessing, Reviewing and Changing Your Personal Information
9. Other Information Collectors
10. Security
11. Privacy Tools
12. Notice

One important issue that is stressed in the Privacy Policy is that eBay cannot be used by children under the age of 18. However, children can use the site if they are supervised by an adult, but they are not allowed to submit any personal information.

Reporting infringements

Due to the number of items for sale on the site, it is impossible for eBay to police every single auction to make sure that none of the rules are being broken. In an effort to preserve the integrity of the site as much as possible, eBay relies to some extent on the community of users to keep an eye out for prohibited, questionable or infringing items. It is in everyone's best interest to monitor the site and maintain its reputation for good quality, legal and genuine products.

 eBay takes a proactive approach to infringements of the rules and they check through as many auctions as possible. If prohibited, questionable or infringing items are listed for sale there is a reasonable chance that it will be spotted and the auction will be stopped. Disciplinary action may then be taken by eBay against the seller.

One avenue for reporting suspect auctions is through the Contact Us form, which can be found by following the Report Problem link on the Security Center page. This form can be used to report a number of issues, including prohibited items. To use the form:

1 Select a category on which you want to report, and select the relevant sub-categories

Contact Us

Start by choosing a category below. In a few simple steps, you will be able to send us your email. In certain cases you may be offered live help.

1.
- Ask about registration, passwords, changing email / User ID
- Ask about bidding or buying
- Ask about selling or billing (for sellers only)
- Report a listing policy violation or prohibited (banned) item
- Report fake eBay emails (spoofs) and unauthorized account activity
- Report problems with other eBay members

2.
- Copying of your listing
- Items that may violate a copyright or are counterfeit
- Listing policy violations (improper keywords, outside links, etc)
- Prohibited (banned) items
- Mature Audience violations
- Fraudulent listings (illegal seller demands, you didn't receive item, etc)

3.
- Seller demanded cash as payment
- Seller demanded wire transfer as payment
- Report unauthorized copies of CDs, software, games, etc.
- Report counterfeit watches, handbags, jewelry, etc.
- You paid but didn't receive your item
- You paid, but your item wasn't as described

Continue >

2 Click Continue to send your report

Getting started

eBay is known for its auctions, which form the bedrock of the site. This chapter looks at the basics of auctions on eBay and shows the type of information that is displayed. It also covers the My eBay section, which is an individual page that can be tailored to your own requirements to keep track of your buying and selling activities on the site.

Covers

Icons

eBay makes extensive use of icons to provide visual shortcuts that indicate the status of various elements on the site. The most commonly used icons are those for eBay members themselves and those that show the trading and feedback status of members.

Member icon

The first icon that you will probably encounter is the new member icon. This shows other members that you are new to the eBay community and are still finding your way. It also shows that you could be a little naive when it comes to some of the finer points of buying and selling on eBay. For most members this is not a problem, since everyone has to start somewhere, but for some it may be an issue. The new member icon stays next to your name for 30 days and then it disappears. The new member icon looks like this:

Another icon you may come across is the Change of User ID icon. This means that the member has changed their original User ID. In most cases this is perfectly legitimate, but it can be used as a way to try and hide a previously bad trading reputation. The Change of User ID icon looks like this:

Feedback icons

Feedback is vital for assessing a seller's, or a buyer's, reputation and there are numerous icons that denote a member's overall feedback rating (that is, the combination of positive and negative feedback). This is done with a star rating system. Once you have an overall positive rating of 10 or over you will receive a yellow star next to your name. This progresses up to a selection of shooting stars, the highest being a red shooting star, which indicates an overall positive feedback rating of 100,000 or over.

Seller icons

Some sellers on eBay dabble with the sale of a handful of items, while others make selling on eBay a full-time occupation. One way to assess the status of a seller is whether they have a Power Seller icon next to their name. The Power Seller icon indicates a high volume of sales each month, and looks like this:

Accessing an auction

Understandably, given the nature of the site, the first thing that most new eBay members want to do is to have a look at an auction. Before jumping in and starting to bid on items, it is a good idea to have a sound understanding of the auction page and how it operates. The first step is to search for items as shown in Chapter One; you will then be able to view the current auctions for matching items:

Item listed here   Current price   Time left

Items that appear at the top of a search results page are known as Featured Items. These are displayed more prominently than subsequent items, but sellers must pay an additional fee for this service. For more information about Featured Items, see Chapter Seven.

1. Click on Buy It Now to purchase an item without having to bid for it. This enables you to buy the item quickly without entering into the auction. However, make sure it is at a price with which you are happy and not more than you would have been prepared to go up to in an auction

Although the Picture Gallery lists all of the items with images, text-only items are also included, but at the very bottom of the list.

2. To view all of the items with images, click on the Picture Gallery link

List View | Picture Gallery

The auction page

Once you have found a specific item in which you are interested, you can access it by clicking on the link next to it on the search results page or on the image (if it has one). This takes you into the auction page for that item. This displays a variety of information about the current auction and enables you to place a bid.

Some auctions have a reserve price attached to them. This is a minimum price that the seller will accept for the item. If the minimum price is not met at the end of the auction then the item will not be sold. The reserve price is not displayed to bidders.

No. of bids so far   Time left   Current high bid

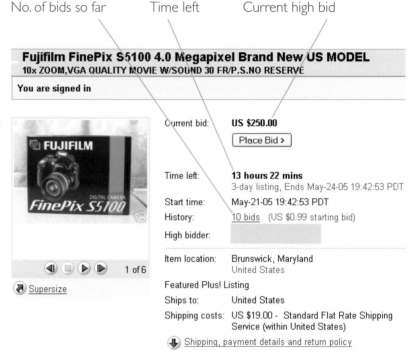

Fujifilm FinePix S5100 4.0 Megapixel Brand New US MODEL
10x ZOOM,VGA QUALITY MOVIE W/SOUND 30 FR/P.S.NO RESERVE

You are signed in

Current bid: **US $250.00**
                 [Place Bid >]

Time left: **13 hours 22 mins**
                 3-day listing, Ends May-24-05 19:42:53 PDT
Start time: May-21-05 19:42:53 PDT
History: 10 bids (US $0.99 starting bid)
High bidder:

Item location: Brunswick, Maryland
                 United States
Featured Plus! Listing
Ships to: United States
Shipping costs: US $19.00 - Standard Flat Rate Shipping
                 Service (within United States)
Shipping, payment details and return policy

1 of 6

Supersize

Don't rush in and bid on the first item you see. Check other similar items and see how much time there is left for a particular auction. It is not a good idea to let other bidders know that you are very keen on a particular item.

Scroll down the page to see a full description of the item and any images that have been posted

Description (revised)
Fujifilm FinePix S5100 4.0 Megapixel
Item Specifics - Digital Cameras

Digital Camera Type:	**SLR, Professional**	Optical Zoom:	**10x**
Digital Camera Brand:	**Fujifilm**	Digital Zoom:	**3.6x**
Product Line:	**Fujifilm FinePix**	Manufacturer Warranty:	**Yes**
Model:	**S5100**	Flash Type:	**Pop-up flash**
Resolution:	**4**	Memory Card Format:	**XD-Picture Card**
Manufacturer Part Number:	**43861100**	Battery Type:	**4 x battery - AA type - alkaline**
Bundled Kits:	–	Condition:	**New, Never Opened**

2 Scroll down the page to view shipping details. You should read these carefully to make sure the seller will post the items to where you live, and also to check that the shipping is not prohibitively expensive

It is particularly important to check the shipping for cheaper items. There is no point in getting a bargain and then having to pay an exorbitant fee in shipping. Some sellers have been known to do this deliberately, to make their item appear more attractively priced and also to avoid paying a higher level of fees, a practice that is prohibited by eBay.

Shipping, payment details and return policy

Shipping Cost	Services Available	Available to
US $19.00	Standard Flat Rate Shipping Service	United States Only

Will ship to United States.

3 Scroll down the page to check the payment details. These will list the ways in which the seller will accept payment for the item

Payment methods accepted

💬 This seller, ▓▓▓▓▓, prefers PayPal.

Learn about payment methods.

Bidding is looked at in greater detail in Chapters Four and Five.

4 If you are happy with all of the details on the auction page and you are still interested in bidding for the item, click on the Place Bid button. This will take you to the next stage of the bidding process and enable you to submit your own bid

`Place Bid >` You will confirm in the next step.

Seller information

At the top-right of the main auction page there is a box containing information about the seller. This is very important as it contains feedback about their previous trading history and it also enables you to contact them directly with any questions you may have about the auction. To access information about a seller:

It is always worthwhile to read a seller's feedback. This not only gives you a good sense of their trading history, it is also a good way to familiarize yourself with the type of feedback that is left on the site.

1 Click here on a seller's User ID to see their full trading profile

2 Click here to read feedback

3 Click here to contact the seller

Seller information

(599 ⭐)

🏋 **Power Seller**

Feedback Score: 599
Positive Feedback: 98.9%
Member since Jul-17-01 in United States

Read feedback comments
Add to Favorite Sellers
Ask seller a question
View seller's other items

4 The seller's full trading profile contains a summary of the feedback that they have received and also a list of the individual comments

Back to your last item   Home > Community > Feedback Forum > **Member Profile**

Member Profile: 🏋 **Power Seller**

		Recent Ratings:			
Feedback Score:	**600**		Past Month	Past 6 Months	Past 12 Months
Positive Feedback:	**98.9%**				
Members who left a positive:	609	➕ positive	27	237	477
Members who left a negative:	7	⊙ neutral	1	6	13
All positive feedback received:	717	➖ negative	0	3	3
Learn about what these numbers mean.		Bid Retractions (Past 6 months): 0			

Feedback Received   From Buyers   From Sellers   Left for Others

743 feedback received by

Comment	From
➕ quick response to all questions, product was in unopened box as promised	Buyer
➕ Camera arrived quickly. Perfect transaction. A++++++++	Buyer
➕ Fast payment,....... A valued ebayer .... A+++	Seller
➕ Good transaction, prompt delivery.	Buyer

My eBay overview

Even if you only have an initial passing interest in eBay, you may be surprised at how quickly you fall under its spell. Before long you may be actively involved in several auctions, keeping a watchful eye on a few more, conducting your own auctions and trying to keep track of all of the financial comings and goings. Trying to keep up with all of this on different pages could become a logistical nightmare, so eBay has introduced a feature to allow members to keep track of all of their online transactions and activities. It is called My eBay and it is like a diary for everything you are involved with on the site. A My eBay page is an invaluable guide for your life on eBay. To begin creating your My eBay page:

Set My eBay as a favorite on your browser, or even as your home page. You will still have to log in to access it, though.

1 Click this link on the main navigation bar

2 A summary of your eBay activities is listed here as well as links to various options within My eBay

3 Click here to view the latest news and announcements from eBay. These are automatically included on My eBay pages when they are released. Each link takes you to the relevant news item or announcement. Since eBay is such an active and evolving site, this is a good way of keeping up with what is happening

My eBay page

As you start becoming more involved with eBay, your My eBay page will contain more items corresponding to your activity on the site. These include details of items you are watching, auctions in which you are involved, items you have won or lost in auctions, and a financial history of your dealings on eBay.

1 When you have won items in an auction, the details will be displayed within the My Summary of your My eBay page:

To change the time period for the Items I've Won section, click on the Period box and select a different time period.

2 This icon denotes that an item has been paid for

If a seller does not leave feedback for you immediately after you have paid for an item, don't panic. Sometimes it takes people a while to respond, and some sellers will only leave feedback once they have received some first.

3 This icon denotes that feedback has been left

4 This icon denotes that feedback has been received

5 Information on how much you have spent on auctions is listed below the auction details

Watching items

Before you start participating in auctions, it is a good idea to have a look at a few that are selling the types of products in which you are interested. This will give you a good idea of the type of condition they are in, the price ranges in which they are sold and the number of bidders there are for certain items. This last point is important because if there are a lot of people interested in a certain type of product then this could result in some keenly fought auctions and, more importantly, some high prices. As part of the research into how certain items are performing it is a good idea to watch a few auctions to see how they progress. Rather than having to do this individually with a lot of different auctions, it is possible to watch multiple auctions from within My eBay. To do this:

Up to 30 items can be listed to be watched at any one time from within the My eBay page.

1 Open an auction in which you are interested

The details of watched items update whenever the My eBay summary page is refreshed in the browser window.

2 Click this link at the top of the auction page

Watch this item in My eBay

To remove a Watched item, tick this box and click the Delete button.

3 The selected auction is displayed on your My eBay page

Comparing auctions

A technique that can be even more useful than watching individual auctions is to compare similar ones side by side. This can be done within the My eBay summary, but a more comprehensive option is to view auctions using the Compare function. To do this:

1 Add two or more items to be watched in My eBay

If you are watching multiple items and you only want to compare some of them, check on the boxes next to them to ensure that these are the only ones included.

2 Click here to compare the auctions in more detail

3 View the details of similar items next to each other. This is an invaluable option for comparing areas such as bid activity, price, shipping costs and payment methods

Another way to compare auctions is to open them in individual browser windows. However, the Compare method is more efficient for a general overview of the items.

Adding notes

Since you may be watching a variety of items for different reasons, it is useful to be able to leave notes next to specific items. These can be used for reminders, for example a time or date at which to bid, or just for general information, such as a suggestion to look up similar items from the same seller when the current auction finishes. To add notes to watched items:

1 Tick the box next to a watched item

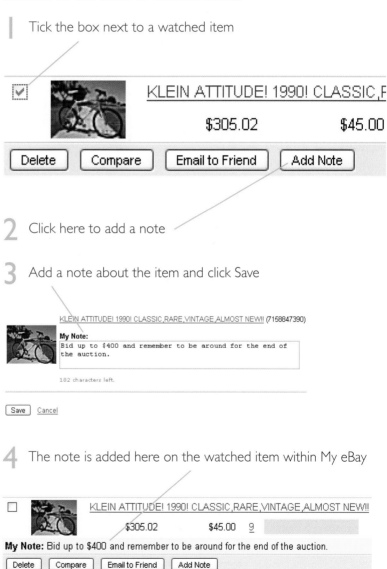

Notes that are left next to items you are watching are visible only to you; no other users can see them.

2 Click here to add a note

3 Add a note about the item and click Save

4 The note is added here on the watched item within My eBay

Viewing won items

Whenever you have completed a successful auction and won an item, the details will be displayed in the My eBay summary. The details displayed here can be customized to increase or decrease the number of columns of information on display:

Details of items you have won are displayed within the My eBay summary. Click here to customize the display

To delete an item from the Items I've Won display, tick the box next to the Seller's ID and click Remove.

Select an item to be included under Item I've Won and click here for it to be displayed

Customize Items I've Won

Available Columns
Start Price
My Max Bid
Shipping Cost

Columns To Display
Qty
Sale Price
Total Price
Paid*
Feedback Left*
Feedback Received*

Move

Seller ID/Seller Email, Title, Sale Date, and Action are required columns and cannot be moved.

*Legend: $ Paid ☆ Feedback Left ○ Feedback Received

Display: seller by their: User ID
Email addresses will be displayed for 14 days after a transaction ends.
☑ My Notes   ☑ eBay Notes
☐ Pictures
10 ▾ items per page
This setting does not apply to the My Summary page.

Custom Period: Show items for last 40 days (60 days max)

Save | Restore Defaults | Cancel

3 Click here to change the order in which the items appear

Customize Items I've Won

Available Columns

Start Price
My Max Bid

Columns To Display

Qty
Sale Price
Total Price
Shipping Cost
Paid*
Feedback Left*
Feedback Received*

Move

Seller ID/Seller Email, Title, Sale Date, and Action are required columns and cannot be moved.

*Legend: $ Paid ☆ Feedback Left ○ Feedback Received

Display: seller by their: [User ID ▾]

Email addresses will be displayed for 14 days after a transaction ends.

☑ My Notes   ☑ eBay Notes
☐ Pictures
[10 ▾] items per page

This setting does not apply to the My Summary page.

Custom Period: Show items for last [40] days (60 days max)

[Save]   Restore Defaults | Cancel

If you include too many categories in the Items I've Won section it may start to look cluttered and difficult to follow. Decide which categories are the most important and stick to them.

4 Click here to save the customized settings

5 Return to the My eBay summary to view the customized items

Items I've Won (1 item)   Customize Display ⊗ ⊗ ⊗

Show: **All** | Awaiting Payment (0) | Awaiting Feedback (1)   Period: [Custom (last 40 days) ▾]

☐	Seller ID	Qty	Sale Price	Total Price	Shipping Cost	Sale Date	Action	$ ☆ ○
☐		1	$0.99	$0.99	$0.00	May-25	[Leave Feedback ▾]	$ ☆ ⊕

3600 RECIPES E-Book Free ship! DELIVERED IN MINUTES! (4382942094)

[Remove] [Add Note]

My eBay favorites

As shown in Chapter One, you can create favorite searches for topics you want to check on regularly. These searches can be accessed from the My eBay page by clicking here:

All Favorites
- Searches
- Sellers
- Categories

It is always worth trying to find a core of favorite sellers who sell the types of products in which you are interested. This can make it quicker when you are looking for specific items and it can also be beneficial to build up a positive business relationship with individual sellers.

In addition to favorite searches, it is also possible to create lists of favorite sellers and categories. If you find a seller you like, and you want to keep an eye on other items that they have coming up for sale, then you can add them as a favorite seller. For categories, you can select a specific category (a particular sub-category of the standard main categories) and view this over time as the items for sale within it change.

Adding favorite sellers

To create a list of favorite sellers:

1 Click on the Sellers link in the All Favorites box above

2 Click on the Add New Seller or Store link in the All Favorites section of the My eBay summary

3 Enter the details of the seller or store to be added to your list of favorite sellers

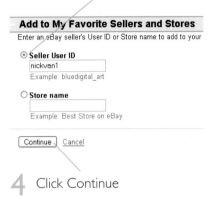

4 Click Continue

5 The seller is added to the All Favorites section within the My eBay summary. Click on the seller's User ID to see the other items which they currently have for sale

Adding favorite categories

To create a list of favorite categories:

1 Click on the Categories link in the All Favorites box in the My eBay summary

2 Click on the Add New Category link

3 Select a main category and drill down through the sub-categories until you reach the item you want

For every category that is selected, a category number should be shown in the box at the top of the window. If not, the category will not be included as a favorite.

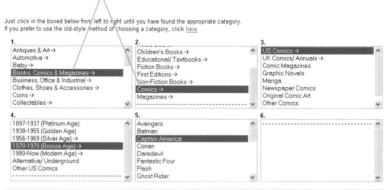

4 Scroll to the bottom of the page and click here to add the category as a favorite

Up to four categories can be added to the Favorite Categories list.

5 The new favorite category can be viewed in the All Favorites section of the My eBay summary

6 Click here to view different options for the selected category, such as current auctions or upcoming ones

Customizing My eBay

Since the My eBay area is your own personal record of your activities on the site, it is only logical that you can customize it to appear the way you want. It is possible to add or remove sections of the My eBay page and also to change the order in which they appear. To customize a My eBay page:

1 Click here at the top of the summary page

If you customize the My Summary page and do not like the end result, click on the Restore Defaults link in the Customize My Summary window to restore it to its original format.

2 Select an item to add to the summary page

Items such as favorite searches can still be viewed independently by clicking on the relevant link in the All Favorites box on the Summary page, but they will only be included permanently in the Summary if they are selected as shown here.

3 Click here to add the selected item. Click Save

4 The selected item is added to the summary page

Rearranging items

If you do not like the order in which items are presented on the My eBay summary page, for example if the one you access most frequently is at the bottom of the page and you have to scroll down to see it, then it is possible to rearrange the order in which they appear. To do this:

It can be beneficial to include elements with the fewest items at the top of the My Summary page. This will enable the items below to be visible without having to scroll down the page.

1 Once an item has been added to the list of items to be included on the summary page, select it in this panel

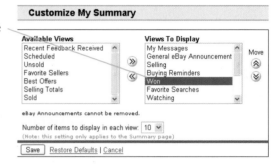

2 Click here to change the item's order. This will effect where it appears on the summary page

3 The item will appear at the selected point on the summary page

Beginning to buy

The fun really starts on eBay when you begin participating in auctions to try to buy items by bidding against other people. The thrill of the chase and the competitive element give auctions an added edge to merely buying items from an online retailer. This chapter looks at how auctions work on eBay, shows some of the details that can be accessed and goes through the whole process of bidding for items.

Covers

Chapter Four

General buying guidelines

Once people have got to grips with the eBay site and the way it functions, the first thing they usually want to do is to start buying things. Even if you are looking at eBay as a source of income through selling, buying is definitely a good starting point: this allows you to participate in the auction process without the additional responsibility of being the seller. It is a good way of interacting with other eBayers and understanding more about the payment and feedback processes. However, before you start buying, there are some general guidelines that should be observed:

- Do some research about the item you want to buy; initially, this can be done on eBay. Resist the temptation to bid for the first similar item you come across when searching on eBay: for most searches you will find several items which could meet your needs. Initially, look at some of them to see the bid amounts they are attracting, what kind of condition they are in, the charge for the shipping and packaging, how the seller would like to receive payment and where they are willing to send it. Compare this with other, similar items so that you can build up a good understanding of what is available. Once you have done this, add several similar items to your Items I'm Watching in My eBay and keep an eye on the auctions until they are finished. Then you will be able to see the final price that each item fetched and also the User ID of the person who has won the bid. This is particularly important if you think you will be bidding for similar items. If you keep a record of another eBayer's bidding activities it may be possible to second-guess how they are going to act if they are participating in the same auction as you at any stage.

A lot of traditional price guides are now being overtaken by eBay itself: the price paid on the site is usually a good reflection of an item's worth.

- Do some research outside eBay. For a lot of items, such as cars and computers, there are trade magazines that offer prices for new and used items. Also, there are a variety of specialist magazines for collectable items that give detailed reports of how much certain items are worth, according to their condition and rarity. Before shopping on eBay it is worth looking at a guide related to the items in which you are interested, to get an idea of their general price.

Make sure you can't buy an item cheaper elsewhere. Although it can be a very enjoyable and worthwhile experience buying items on eBay, there is little point in doing so if you can buy the same thing cheaper in one of your local shops. Before plunging into eBay, have a look around locally to see if similar items are available and, if so, the price at which they are sold.

Establish whether you are happy with second-hand goods or if you want everything to be brand new. Some people love the thought of getting a bargain with a second-hand item, while others would never entertain the idea. This is a personal decision, and on eBay there are both new and used goods: check the description to see if an item is new or second-hand.

Don't enter into an auction just for the sake of it. Sometimes when browsing through eBay you may look at something just out of interest or curiosity. Once the auction page is visible there can be a desire to place a bid just to try and win it. If possible, resist this and always ask yourself if you really want, or need, a particular item.

Contacting the seller is a good way to establish a rapport with other people in the eBay community and can help you feel more confident in your transactions.

Establish a maximum price you are prepared to pay for an item and stick to it. Once an auction starts it is easy to get carried away and let the competitive nature of the process develop into a "win-at-all-costs" attitude. This is fine if you are determined to acquire an item but there is little point in winning if you pay too much as a result. For most items, similar auctions will be available soon.

Avoid jumping in with a very high, early bid. Novice bidders frequently put in high bids as soon as they see an auction, in their desire to try and secure it. This not only puts them at a disadvantage (because other people can see that they are overly keen) but it is also unnecessary: if an auction has several days to go it is better to watch and see how the bidding is progressing before you enter the fray. If you put in a bid near to the closing time then there is less chance for other people to outbid you.

Buy It Now option

Although eBay is known primarily as an auction site, there is also a facility for buying items immediately from a seller, without using the bidding process. This is know as Buy It Now (BIN). The Buy It Now option can be used in two ways: in conjunction with an auction, in which case the BIN option is removed once the first auction bid has been placed; or on its own, which results in a transaction that is the same as any non-auction online retailer.

If it is used in conjunction with an auction, the BIN price is usually pitched at just over what the seller thinks they may get in the auction itself. For the buyer there could be several reasons to buy an item using the BIN option:

Placing a starting bid on an auction that also has a Buy It Now price is known as BIN Stomping. This is done by buyers to remove the BIN price and hopefully acquire the item at a significantly lower price.

- They want the item as soon as possible and do not want to wait until the auction ends, which could be several days.

- They are happy with the price as it is less than they would have gone up to in the auction itself.

- They do not want the unpredictability of an auction.

To buy an item using the Buy It Now option:

If a Buy It Now sale does not also have an auction option, this is known as a Fixed Price format. This means that the item can only be bought at the stated price. To sell with this option you must have an overall feedback rating of 10 or higher, or a direct debit facility on file with eBay, or a PayPal account and an overall feedback rating of 5 or more.

1 Locate an item that is on sale for a BIN price

☐ 📷 3600 RECIPES E-Book Free ship! DELIVERED IN MINUTES!   🅿 $0.99 *Buy It Now*

2 Access the item and click this button

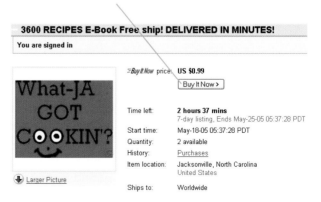

3600 RECIPES E-Book Free ship! DELIVERED IN MINUTES!
You are signed in

Buy It Now price: **US $0.99**

Buy It Now >

Time left:	**2 hours 37 mins**
	7-day listing, Ends May-25-05 05:37:28 PDT
Start time:	May-18-05 05:37:28 PDT
Quantity:	2 available
History:	Purchases
Item location:	Jacksonville, North Carolina United States
Ships to:	Worldwide

Larger Picture

3 Check the purchase details and click here

Buy It Now

Hello nickvan1! (Not you?) Enter the quantity you'd like to buy and click **Continue**.

Item title: **3600 RECIPES E-Book Free ship! DELIVERED IN MINUTES!**

Buy It Now price: **US $0.99**

Quantity: **x** [1]

[Continue >]   You will confirm in the next step.

Purchase this item now without bidding.
Learn about Buy It Now.

The Buy It Now option is useful for items such as presents, when you want something for a particular time and you do not want the uncertainty of an auction.

4 Click here to purchase the item

Review and Commit to Buy

Hello nickvan1! (Not you?)

Item title:	3600 RECIPES E-Book Free ship! DELIVERED IN MINUTES!
Buy It Now price:	**US $0.99**
Shipping and handling:	Free - Standard Flat Rate Shipping Service (within United States).
Payment methods:	PayPal, Personal check, Money order/Cashiers check.

By clicking on the button below, you commit to buy this item from the seller.

[Commit to Buy]   Only click the **Commit to Buy** button **once**. Processing may take a few moments.

5 Confirmation of the sale is displayed

The payment process for a Buy It Now item is the same as for an item won in an auction. For more details about paying for items, see Chapter Ten.

6 Click here to proceed to the payment section for the item

7 Once the item has been purchased you will receive notification on eBay and an email confirming the details

Multiple item auctions

Multiple item auctions, also known as Dutch auctions, are ones where a seller has several identical items for sale. Instead of selling them all in individual auctions they can choose to sell them as separate lots in a single auction. So if someone has 20 identical bicycles for sale they can list them in a single auction. The buyers can then put in a bid and also specify the quantity that they wish to buy. So someone could bid $50.00 and specify that they would like a quantity of three. If this is the final highest bid then they would pay $150.00 for the three bicycles ($50.00 each). In a multiple item auction, all of the highest winning bidders pay the same price. So in this example the next 17 highest bidders would also be able to purchase a bicycle for $50.00.

Multiple item auctions work in a similar way to single item auctions, with the exception that the current high bid is determined by the price offered multiplied by the quantity ordered. So someone bidding $10.00 and asking for a quantity of three would have a higher bid than someone bidding $25.00 and asking for a quantity of one.

Although multiple item auctions are a perfectly legitimate part of eBay, they do not always find great support from sellers. This is because they have to sell all of the items at the same price. A more common occurrence is for sellers to list multiple items with just a Buy It Now price. Buyers can then buy one or more of the items at a set price: the seller knows exactly how much they are going to get for each item and the buyer can order as many items as they want at this set price.

1 Multiple item auctions at a set Buy It Now price are now a regular feature on eBay

2 The number of items available is listed here and buyers can purchase one or more

How an auction works

An auction on eBay is similar in some ways to one held in an auction house, in that the person who places the highest bid is the one who secures the item. However, since eBay auctions operate in an online environment, there are two important differences.

The first difference with an eBay auction is that users can place bids that are higher than the current price of an item (typically the top price that they are prepared to pay) and eBay will automatically bid up to this maximum price. For example, if the current high bid is $1 and someone then bids a maximum of $10, the current high bid moves up to $1.25. If no-one else bids on the item then the bidder will get it for this price, rather than the $10 maximum. However, if someone else bids on the item, eBay will keep raising the current high bid up to the maximum bid by the first bidder. So if a second bidder comes in with a maximum bid of $3, eBay will raise the current high bid to $3.25 for the first bidder. To become the high bidder, the second bidder will have to put in a bid of over $10, i.e. the first bidder's maximum price. This form of bidding is known as proxy bidding, which means that eBay will bid automatically on your behalf up to the maximum you have stated when you first bid.

You never see the maximum amount that someone has bid, only the current high bid. In some cases this may be the same, but not necessarily.

When a proxy bid is placed it goes up by a specific incremental level. The increment depends on the amount of the bid and these incremental levels are displayed on the following page.

When looking at the duration of an auction for an item in which you are interested, try to make sure you will be around at the end of the auction. This will enable you to make a last minute bid, if required.

The second difference with an eBay auction is that it is for a set duration. Currently, the maximum duration for an auction is 10 days and the minimum is 1 day. The duration of an auction is set by the seller at the time of listing the item. Some points to consider when looking at the duration of an auction are:

● If the duration is too short then people may miss the auction

● If there are several days to go for an auction there is no need to place a bid immediately. Wait and see how the auction progresses and then bid accordingly.

● If you are unavailable when the auction finishes you can place a maximum bid and let eBay place proxy bids on your behalf.

Bidding increments

The amount by which a high bid increases once someone bids above it is set by eBay. The current incremental bid levels are:

Prices given in this book were correct at the time of going to press.

- If the current high bid is between $0.01 and $0.99 the increment level is $0.05 (so that, if the current high bid is $1 and someone bids a maximum of $5, the current high bid would go up to $1.05)

- If the current high bid is between $1.00 and $4.99 the incremental level is $0.25

Bidding increments determine the minimum amount someone has to bid over the current high bid to become the new high bidder. If you try to put in a bid that is under the next incremental level, eBay will not let you.

- If the current high bid is between $5.00 and $24.99 the incremental level is $0.50

- If the current high bid is between $25.00 and $99.99 the incremental level is $1.00

- If the current high bid is between $100.00 and $249.99 the incremental level is $2.50

- If the current high bid is between $250.00 and $499.99 the incremental level is $5.00

- If the current high bid is between $500.00 and $999.99 the incremental level is $10.00

- If the current high bid is between $1000.00 and $2,499.99 the incremental level is $25.00

- If the current high bid is between $2,500.00 and $4,999.99 the incremental level is $50.00

- If the current high bid is over $5,000.00 the incremental level is $100.00

Since the incremental levels are dependant on the current high bid, these can change as an auction progresses e.g. if the high bid is $10 the incremental level will be more than if it was $2.

Example auction

When you start bidding in auctions the proxy system and incremental levels can be a bit confusing. It is always worth watching a few auctions to see how the high bid is arrived at and then, when the auction finishes, you can view all of the bids. If in doubt, start by bidding on auctions for low-priced items. The following example shows how a standard auction operates using the proxy system and bidding incremental levels:

Some sellers set a reserve price for an item. This is a minimum amount which they are prepared to accept for an item. If the reserve is not met then they do not have to sell. There are advantages and disadvantages in having a reserve price and this is looked at in more detail in Chapter Seven.

- A seller lists an item for sale at $1.00. This is known as the starting price and is the minimum price someone has to bid to become the high bidder and have the current high bid.

- Bidder A makes a bid of $1.00, known as the starting bid. The current high bid is therefore $1.00.

- Bidder B wants to make a bid and sees that they have to bid a minimum of $1.25 (the incremental level up for an item at this price). Bidder B does this, and becomes the high bidder with a current high bid of $1.25.

- Bidder C wants to up the bidding. They see the next bid is $1.50 or more (since the item has an incremental level of $0.25). However, they want to make a more significant bid and so bid a maximum of $16.00. They become the current high bidder and the current high bid is $1.50: the next incremental level above the previous high bid.

- Bidder B sees that they have been outbid and that the next bid has to be $1.75 or higher. They place a bid of $2.00 but receive a message to say that they have been outbid. This is because Bidder C's maximum has not been reached, so eBay places a proxy bid on their behalf. This raises the current high bid to $2.25: Bidder B's bid of $2.00 plus the next incremental level of $0.25. Bidder C is still the current high bidder.

- Bidder B still wants the item and sees that the current high bid has to be $2.50 or higher (the current high bid plus the next increment level of $0.25). They decide to place a bid of $6.00, but again receive a message to say that they have been outbid. Once more, eBay has placed a proxy bid for Bidder B, since Bidder C's bid has not yet matched Bidder B's maximum bid. So the current high bid becomes Bidder C's bid plus the next incremental level (which has now risen to $0.50 as the current high bid is over $5.00). So the new current high bid is $6.00 plus $0.50, making $6.50.

Although it can be frustrating to be outbid in an auction, don't get into a bidding war just to beat someone else. You may end up winning the auction, but at an inflated price.

● At this point Bidder B decides to drop out of the auction. Although they can see the current high bid, they do not know Bidder C's maximum bid (as this is not displayed). They therefore decide that they are not prepared to pay more.

● Bidder A now re-enters the auction. They have been watching it progress since the beginning and wanted to wait until a few bids had been made until they made another bid. They now realize that Bidder C is an experienced operator and has probably put in a fairly high maximum bid. Bidder A therefore puts in a bid of $19.00. This surpasses Bidder C's maximum bid of $16.00 and so Bidder A becomes the current high bidder. The current high bids becomes $16.50, which is Bidder C's maximum plus the increment at this price point of $0.50. (Bidder A could have become the current high bidder with a bid of $16.01 but they had no way of knowing Bidder C's maximum bid.)

● Bidder C now has a difficult decision to make. They know that Bidder A is a serious bidder and they have to decide how badly they really want the item and how much they are prepared to spend. The current amount they would have to bid is $19.50: the current high bid plus the incremental amount of $0.50. Bidder C places a bid of $26.00, making the current high bid $19.50: Bidder A's maximum bid of $19.00 plus the $0.50 increment.

It is perfectly acceptable to watch an auction for several days and then come in with a bid at the last moment. Bidding strategies are looked at in more detail in Chapter Five.

● Bidder A realizes that they have serious competition. Because of this, they wait until the last few minutes of the auction and put in a final bid of $30.00. They win the auction and the final price is $27.00: Bidder C's final maximum bid of $26.00 plus the next incremental level of $1.00.

Bidding history

There are certain details that can be ascertained from watching an auction. One of these is the bidding history for a particular item. This can be useful as it shows who has been bidding and how many bids they have had to make to become, or try to become, the highest bidder. To view the bidding history:

Looking at the bidding history can be a good way of getting to know the habits of other people in the auction. For instance, someone might bid at the same time each day; someone else might make a number of consecutive bids in order to become the current high bidder. This can be useful information when it comes to bidding tactics, particularly towards the end of an auction.

1 Open the auction page and click here

2 The current highest bidder is displayed here. The date displayed is when the current high bid was placed. The high bid is not necessarily the maximum bid by the high bidder, just the maximum required to beat any other current bids

Whenever you put in a bid it will be registered in the bidding history, even if you do not become the high bidder. This is because you can automatically be outbid if someone else has put in a higher maximum. So, in effect, your bid would be the high bidder for a split second until the proxy bid is placed by eBay. Therefore it is possible to have several bids appear consecutively in the bidding history, without once becoming the high bidder.

3 All bids that did not beat the high bidder are shown below it. Look at the times to see when these bids

User ID	Bid Amount	Date of bid
nickvan1 (15 ☆) me	US $875.67	May-22-05 07:25:00 PDT
	US $865.67	May-20-05 11:01:53 PDT
	US $856.00	May-22-05 07:24:48 PDT
	US $820.00	May-22-05 07:24:39 PDT
	US $800.00	May-20-05 08:05:23 PDT
	US $700.00	May-20-05 01:00:47 PDT
	US $675.00	May-20-05 08:04:37 PDT
	US $650.00	May-20-05 08:04:08 PDT
	US $590.00	May-20-05 06:38:24 PDT
	US $570.00	May-19-05 22:49:48 PDT
	US $500.00	May-19-05 22:31:20 PDT

were made. In some cases, several bids can be made one after another but they still do not beat the highest bid, so the bidder tries again

Bidding in an auction

The majority of sales on eBay are still done through auctions. This chapter looks at the bidding process and shows how to develop a strategy to try to give yourself as good a chance as possible of winning items in which you are interested. It also covers asking the seller a question and retracting a bid if you have made a mistake.

Covers

Chapter Five

Bidding for an item

Once you have done all of your research, and understand fully the way in which the bidding works, it is time to start participating in an auction. This is the essence of eBay and it can be an exciting and stimulating experience. But be careful not to get too carried away. To start bidding for an item:

Start by bidding for some lower-priced items, to give yourself a chance to get to know how the system works.

1 Find the item in which you are interested and open the auction page. Check the details and, if you are happy with them, click here to start bidding for the item

BRAND NEW APPLE IPOD SHUFFLE 512MB MP3 PLAYER
You are signed in

Current bid: **US $80.00** (Reserve met)
[Place Bid >]

Time left: **56 mins 49 secs**
7-day listing, Ends May-25-05 20:50 PDT
Start time: May-18-05 05:20:50 PDT
History: 11 bids (US $39.00 starting bid)
High bidder: (0)
Item location: Hong Kong, 852
Hong Kong
Ships to: Worldwide
Shipping costs: US $12.00 - Standard Flat Rate Shipping Service (within United States)
Other shipping services available

Shipping, payment details and return policy

Larger Picture

2 The amount of the current high bid is shown at the top of the page. To become the high bidder you have to beat this price by at least the next incremental step in the auction

Matching the next incremental level shown on the Place a Bid page does not guarantee you will become the current high bidder. This depends on the maximum amount bid by other users.

Place a Bid

Hello nickvan1! (Not you?) Enter your maximum bid and click **Continue**.

Item title: BRAND NEW APPLE IPOD SHUFFLE 512MB MP3 PLAYER

Current bid: US $80.00

Your maximum bid: US $ [81.59]   (Enter US $81.00 **or more**)

[Continue >]   You will confirm in the next step.

eBay automatically bids on your behalf **up to** your maximum bid.
Learn about bidding.

3 Enter the maximum amount that you are prepared to bid at this point. The minimum amount required is shown to the right of the bid amount box. Click the Continue button to move to the next step of the bidding process

Make sure you review your bid carefully and that you have typed the correct amount. Mistakes can be rectified later but it is better to get it right first time.

4 Check the details of your bid carefully

— Review and Confirm Bid

Hello nickvan1! (Not you?)	
Item title:	BRAND NEW APPLE IPOD SHUFFLE 512MB MP3 PLAYER
Your maximum bid:	**US $81.59**
Shipping and handling:	US $12.00 - Standard Flat Rate Shipping Service (within United States). Additional services available.
Payment methods:	PayPal

By clicking on the button below, you commit to buy this item from the seller if you're the winning bidder.

[Confirm Bid]
---

5 Click Confirm Bid to enter your bid

Once a bid has been made and confirmed, there is a binding legal contract between the buyer and the seller.

6 If your bid is above the next incremental level of the current high bid then you will become the current high bidder. If this is the case, a Bid Confirmation box appears on the auction page:

Bid Confirmation

You are signed in

 You are the current high bidder (the reserve price has been met)

> **Important:** You are one bid away from being outbid. If another user places a bid, you will not win. To increase your chances of winning, enter your highest maximum bid.

Title: BRAND NEW APPLE IPOD SHUFFLE 512MB MP3 PLAYER

Time left:	51 mins 29 secs
History:	12 bids
Current bid:	US $81.00 (Reserve met)
Your maximum bid:	**US $81.59**

[Enter Higher Maximum Bid]   or   Check your status
Increase your chances of winning   See if you're still the high bidder

7 If your bid is not higher than the current high bidder's maximum, the following page will be displayed. Click here if you want to submit another, higher bid

If you see that you have been outbid by a proxy bid (a bid made automatically by eBay because someone else has put in a higher maximum bid), review your own bidding strategy, particularly in light of the maximum you are willing to pay for the item. Once the price reaches your own limit, stop bidding. You can always check the final price at the end of the auction by visiting the auction page.

8 Once you have become the high bidder, the current high bid is displayed here (this is not necessarily your maximum bid)

Current bid: **US $81.00 (Reserve met)**

Place Bid >

Time left: **47 mins 19 secs**
7-day listing, Ends May-25-05 05:20:50 PDT
Start time: May-18-05 05:20:50 PDT
History: 12 bids (US $39.00 starting bid)
High bidder: nickvan1 (15 ☆) me

9 Your User ID is displayed here as the high bidder

Viewing high bidder details

Once you have become the high bidder for an item, you can check in a number of ways that you haven't been outbid:

1 Click on the Bid History link on the auction home page. Your name should be displayed at the top of the list

Bid History   Item number

Maximum bid: US $81.59   Email to a friend | **Watch this item**

Item title: BRAND NEW APPLE IPOD SHUFFLE 512MB MP3 PLAYER
Time left: 45 minutes 20 seconds

Only actual bids (not automatic bids generated up to a bidder's maximum) are shown. A bids may be placed days or hours before a listing ends. Learn more about bidding.

User ID	Bid Amount	Date of bid
nickvan1 (15 ☆) me	US $81.00	May-25-05 04:29:21 PDT
	US $80.00	May-24-05 20:10:52 PDT
	US $80.00	May-24-05 23:42:22 PDT

Even when you are the current high bidder, it is a good idea to check the bid history to see what bidding activity has gone on and who is involved in the auction.

2 You will be sent an email telling you about your high bidder status and giving details of the item

You Are the Current High Bidder

Dear nickvan1,
You are currently the high bidder for the following eBay item from mickel18.

Bid details
Item name:	BRAND NEW APPLE IPOD SHUFFLE 512MB MP3 PLAYER
Item number:	
Seller:	
Quantity:	1
Your current bid:	US $81.00
Your maximum bid:	US $81.59
Current price:	US $81.00 **(reserve met)**
End Date:	25-May-05 13:20:50 BST

The price for items that you are winning in an auction are shown in green on the My eBay page. Items for which you have currently been outbid show the price in red.

3 The item will be added to your My eBay page, under the Items I'm Bidding On section

Items I'm Bidding On (1 item)   Customize Display ⊗ ⊗ ⊗
Show: **All** | Winning (1) | Not Winning (0)

	Picture	Current Price	My Max Bid	Shipping Cost	Time Left △	Action
☐	🖼	BRAND NEW APPLE IPOD SHUFFLE 512MB MP3 PLAYER				View Seller's Other Items ▼
		$81.00	$81.59	$12.00	43m	

Add Note

Being outbid

Even if you are the current highest bidder for an item, you can still be outbid later by another user. This just means that someone else will have put in a bid which is higher than the maximum figure you entered.

If this happens, you are notified about it in two ways:

1 On the auction page, a notice appears to alert you to the fact that you have been outbid. Click here to place another bid

eBay always makes it as easy as possible for you to place another bid once you have been outbid.

2 An email is sent to you detailing the fact that you have been outbid. Click here to place another bid

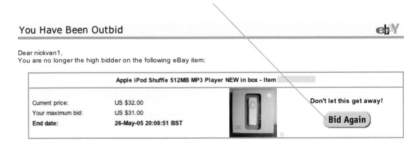

Asking questions

During an auction there may be questions that you would like to ask the seller. These could involve the condition of the item, the shipping details, or a specific question about something in the description of the item. If there is anything that you want to ask it is essential that you do so: after the auction has ended it will be too late. When you receive an answer to your question, if there is anything that you are still unsure about then ask another question. There is no limit to the number of questions you can ask a seller, but apply some common sense when doing so and do not bombard them with unnecessary queries. To ask a seller a question:

Ask questions before you place a bid rather than afterwards, when it may be too late.

1. Access the auction page and click here in the Seller Information box

Seller information

Feedback Score: 2
Positive Feedback: 100%
Member since Nov-18-99 in Hong Kong

Read feedback comments
Add to Favorite Sellers
Ask seller a question
View seller's other items

Safe Buying Tips

If you do not get an answer to a question then you should not proceed with bidding for the item. This could be an indication that there is a problem with this particular seller.

2. Click here and select the type of question you want to ask

Question about how to pay for this item

What are the exact methods of payment that you accept for this item.

932 characters left. HTML cannot be displayed.

☑ Send me a copy of this question.

☑ Add this item to my watch list.

Submit question   Cancel

3. Enter your question here and click the Submit Question button

Bidding to win

No one likes losing an auction, particularly if it is for an item that you really want. With experience you will get to develop your own bidding strategies, but some simple tactics can give you a significant advantage over other bidders:

- Don't jump in too early with a high bid. When you first view an auction, look to see when it finishes. If it is several days until the end (and you know you will be around to watch the auction) there is no need to place a bid. Instead, just watch the auction to see what activity is taking place. See who else is bidding and by how much the current high bid is increasing.

- Test the water. Once you have watched an auction for a few days place an initial bid to see what response it gets. Then watch to see if any higher bids come in. If they do, then you know you have competition. At this point it is best to watch the auction again for a while: there is no point in getting into a bidding war at an early stage, as this could enable someone else to come in with a higher bid once you have reached your maximum bid. Ideally, you want to be able to come in with your highest bid as close to the end of the auction as possible.

- Enter uneven numerical values. One mistake that a lot of novice eBay bidders make is to bid in round figures – $5.00, $10.00, $200.00, etc. While this may seem logical, it makes it easier for more experienced eBayers to win the auction by only a few pence. For instance, if someone bids $5.03 rather than $5.00 then they could become the current high bidder because of the extra three cents. Always add odd figures like this to the end of bids, as it increases your chances of outbidding people who use round figures.

- Check out the opposition. Watch the bid history of an item to see if other bidders bid at a particular time. For instance, someone may bid in the evening after work, whereas someone else may work night shifts and so bid during the afternoon. If people bid near the end of an auction then you know that they will probably be watching it right up to the closing time.

If another user bids back immediately after you have placed a bid then it is a sign that they are keen on the item. If there are a few days left for the auction, you do not need to place another bid immediately.

● Make sure you are in a position to make a bid towards the end of the auction. If you know you are not going to be near your own computer when the auction is due to finish, try to make alternative arrangements: if there is a friend or relation who could place a bid on your behalf then give them details of what to do and how much to bid. Otherwise try and access eBay from another computer.

● Refresh your browser regularly when watching an auction. The time left is only updated if you refresh your browser window; it does not happen automatically.

Don't be tempted to increase the maximum you are prepared to pay for an item just because someone else has outbid you.

● Enter your maximum bid towards the end of the auction. If you have been following an auction and it has still not reached the maximum which you are prepared to pay then you can enter this amount with hours, or preferably minutes, left on the auction. If you become the high bidder it does not mean that you will necessarily have to pay your maximum amount, as the current high bid will go up to the next increment above the previous high bid. There is no point in putting your maximum bid in at the beginning of an auction, as this just gives other bidders a target to aim for and several days to do so. Bidding at the last moment in an auction is known as "sniping" and this is looked at on page 84.

● Don't panic if you get into a bidding war with someone else. This can be one of the most exciting aspects of eBay but it is important not to get carried away. Don't keep bidding just for the sake of it: if the price goes above the maximum you have decided on, then stop bidding (although it can be worth going over it by a small amount, just in case). If you want to keep bidding, don't enter a bid immediately after someone else has outbid you. Evaluate the bid that has been made and check the bid history to see how often the current high bidder has bid. Also, check the time left for the auction: if it is still a few days then you can happily stop bidding at this point and wait until the auction is nearer the end. A cool head is often successful when bidding on eBay.

View the bidding history of other users

If you find you are frequently bidding against the same people (which can happen if you are buying the same types of items) then it is a good idea to try and find out as much about their bidding habits as possible. To do this:

1 Access the Advanced Search page and click here to search for details about a specific eBay member. You will have to know their User ID in order to continue with the search

Search

Items
- **Find Items**
  - By eBay Motors Categories
  - Items by Seller
  - Items by Bidder
  - By Item Number

Stores
- Items in Stores
- Find Stores

Members
- Find a Member
- Find Contact Information

Other eBayers will probably be checking your bidding history too. Try to keep them on their toes by bidding at irregular times and try to avoid creating consistent bidding patterns.

2 Enter the User ID click Search. This will take you to the User's ID. Click on their User ID to view their feedback history

Enter User ID or email address of member

nickvan1

Enter the User ID or email address of the mem

Enter a User ID to access a member's profile, i to help you find the member you are looking for address. Learn more.

3 From the user's feedback, click on a link to view items that they have won

[Search]

Feedback Received	From Buyers	From Sellers	Left for Others			
15 feedback received by nickvan1 (0 mutually withdrawn)						Page 1 of 1
Comment				From	Date / Time	Item #
Great buyer...prompt payment, valued customer, highly recommended.				Seller	May-25-05 03:17	4362942094
Item delivered speedily and in good condition. Good contact too.				Buyer	Oct-31-04 11:28	3845558689
good value ,good fast delevery ,hope to buisness again.thanks				Buyer	Oct-22-04 13:39	5129119519
great buyer, fast payment, good transaction - thanks				Seller	Oct-16-04 12:20	7106465761
Prompt PayPal payment, Clear comms, Cant get better. "lotz4you" recommends A+++				Seller	Oct-14-04 15:09	2494249907

4 Click here to view the bid history of the item

Winning bid:	**US $81.00** (Reserve met)
Ended:	May-25-05 05:20:50 PDT
Start time:	May-18-05 05:20:50 PDT
History:	12 bids (US $39.00 starting bid)
Winning bidder:	nickvan1 (17 ☆) me
Item location:	Hong Kong, 852 Hong Kong
Ships to:	Worldwide
Shipping costs:	US $12.00 - Standard Flat Rate

⬇ Larger Picture

Some buyers always put in their first bid when there are only a few seconds of an auction left. If you find you are up against someone like this you will have to try to beat them at their own game by timing your bid even more close to the end of the auction.

5 Study the bid history for the auction that has ended. The final bid amount does not necessarily relate to the maximum bid that was entered. The important item is the Date of Bid column. Check to see the time of the final bid and compare this with the closing time of the auction (see previous image). This will give you an idea of the user's bidding habits and how closely they watch auctions

Item title: BRAND NEW APPLE IPOD SHUFFLE 512MB MP3 PLAYER

Time left: Auction has ended.

Only actual bids (not automatic bids generated up to a bidder's maximum) are shown. Autom placed days or hours before a listing ends. Learn more about bidding.

User ID	Bid Amount	Date of bid
nickvan1 (17 ☆) me	US $81.00	May-25-05 04:29:21 PDT
	US $80.00	May-24-05 20:10:52 PDT
	US $80.00	May-24-05 23:42:22 PDT
	US $70.00	May-24-05 20:10:40 PDT
	US $67.00	May-24-05 08:29:46 PDT
	US $60.00	May-24-05 12:48:02 PDT
	US $55.00	May-24-05 08:29:30 PDT
	US $51.51	May-23-05 11:25:24 PDT
	US $50.00	May-24-05 08:29:16 PDT
	US $47.00	May-24-05 08:29:07 PDT
	US $45.00	May-24-05 06:32:31 PDT

Sniping

The best way to try to win an auction is to put in a bid at the last moment and hope that it is high enough to become the current high bid. If this is the case, it will not give other bidders time to respond. In eBay terminology this is known as "sniping". Although some sellers do not like this practice, as they feel it means buyers do not make as many bids against each other as they could, it is perfectly legitimate and allowable within the eBay rules and regulations. It is also great fun.

When participating in sniping, remember:

A cable or DSL Internet connection should enable you to put in a bid in the last few seconds of an auction. With a dial-up connection you may want to give it a couple of minutes. However, with both methods there is a chance of missing the end of the auction if there is a lot of Internet traffic at that time.

- A fast Internet connection will enable you to leave your bid closer to the end of an auction.

- If you are sniping on an auction then other people may be doing the same. Always be prepared to be out-sniped.

If you want to make a bid at the very last moment, keep one browser window open with the current high bid and time left displayed. Then open another window and enter a final bid. Keep this ready at the submit stage until the last moment. You can still view the current bidding activity and time left, and then send your final bid just before the auction closes:

If you are going to be sniping manually, it is vital that you are at your computer, or can access eBay, at the time when an auction in which you are interested is due to finish.

By keeping two browser windows open for the same auction you can have a bid ready and also view the latest high bid

Automated sniping

Rather than having to sit at your computer and wait for the end of every auction in which you are interested, just so you can put in a snipe bid, it is also possible to use an automated sniping tool to do the work for you. These are online services that will place a bid for you on eBay at a time predetermined by you. After that you can turn off your computer, sit back, put your feet up and wait and see if the sniping software has won the item for you. There are a few points to bear in mind when using sniping software:

Although automated sniping software takes some of the fun out of bidding, it can be a very effective way of winning auctions.

- As with most things connected with computers, sniping software does not always work perfectly. Bids can be missed, or made at the wrong time, although this is a very rare event.

- There is a fee for most sniping software services, usually based on the amount of use or as a flat fee per month.

Some online sniping service include:

- BidRobot at www.bidrobot.com

Even automated sniping tools are subject to delays due to Internet traffic, which could have an impact on a bid that is timed to be placed a few seconds before the end of an auction.

- Cricketsniper at www.cricketsniper.com

- AuctionSniper at www.auctionsniper.com

- AuctionBytes at www.auctionbytes.com (this contains an overview of most sniping sites and links to them)

An online sniping site is worth thinking about if you keep losing auctions in the last few minutes or seconds.

Retracting a bid

Except for a handful of circumstances, a bid on eBay is a legal contract. This means that the buyer is obligated to pay the seller the price of the winning bid and the seller has to provide the buyer with the item in the auction. In general, eBay frowns upon people retracting their bids and will only allow it in certain circumstances. Some of the reasons for which eBay will not allow a bid to be retracted is if a buyer decides that they do not really want an item once they have bid for it, or if they find the same item for cheaper elsewhere. The circumstances under which eBay will allow a bid to be retracted are:

● If you mistakenly enter the wrong amount for a bid; for example if you enter $100.00 instead of $10.00.

● The description of an item does not match the product.

● You cannot reach the seller once the auction has finished.

To retract a bid:

Open the auction page and click here to view the bidding history

Before you retract a bid due to lack of contact with the seller, you have to make a reasonable effort at contacting them – something more than one unanswered telephone call. If in doubt, contact eBay and ask their advice.

Current bid: **US $81.00 (Reserve met)**

Place Bid >

Time left: **26 mins 49 secs**
7-day listing, Ends May-25-05 05:20:50 PDT

Start time: May-18-05 05:20:50 PDT

History: 12 bids (US $39.00 starting bid)

High bidder: nickvan1 (15 ☆) me

2 Click here at the bottom of the Bid History page

User ID	Bid Amount
nickvan1 (**15** ☆) me	US $81.00
	US $80.00
	US $80.00
	US $70.00
	US $67.00
	US $60.00
	US $55.00
	US $51.51
	US $50.00
	US $47.00
	US $45.00
	US $40.50

If you and another bidder placed the same bid amount, the earlier bid takes priority. You can retract your bid under certain circumstances only.

Always double-check the amount that you enter when you place a bid. This will reduce the possibility of having to retract the bid as the result of a mistake or mistyping.

3 Read the information about bid retractions carefully. This should be seen as a last resort and, even though it is relatively easy to do in the right circumstances, it is not something that you should abuse or overuse. Even if you manage to retract your bid there is always a chance that someone might give you negative feedback as a result. Click here to access the Bid Retraction form

How To Retract a Bid

To retract a bid, use the Bid Retraction form.

Note: There is no equivalent for bid retraction in Buy It Now listings. Once you've confirmed your purchase, you are obligated to pay the seller.

The Item Number is displayed on the main auction page for each item.

4 Enter the number of the item for which you placed a bid and select a reason for the retraction

Before you retract your bid, please <u>read complete information</u> on bid retractions

Item number of auction in question:

```
12345678
```

Your explanation of the retraction:

Entered wrong amount	▾

If you have a valid reason not listed above, you can:
Contact the seller and ask the seller to cancel the bid, or contact <u>Rules & Safety</u>

[Retract bid]

Bid retraction is annoying not only for the seller but also for other people who may have bid in the same auction. This is because your retraction could alter the dynamics of the whole auction.

5 Click the Retract Bid button

6 All of the bids that you have placed for the item are retracted, not just the one that was made in error. Conformation of the bid retraction appears after the Retract Bid button is clicked

Bid Retracted

Every bid you have placed on item #   has been cancelled, and your explanation has been recorded.

Bid retraction details also appear on your own User ID profile page.

7 Once a bid has been retracted, these details are displayed at the bottom of the Bid History page, for everyone to see

Bid retraction and cancellation history

User ID	Action / Explanation
<u>nickvan1</u> (<u>6</u>)	**Retracted:** **Explanation:**Entered wrong bid amount

8 If a bid is retracted because of entering the wrong amount you have to go back to the auction and enter the bid that you intended to place initially. If not you will incur the displeasure of eBay and perhaps end up with negative feedback from the seller

Winning an auction

A lot of experienced eBayers leave their bidding until the final hours or minutes of an auction. This gives them a chance to see the pattern of the bidding and who is involved in the auction. For this reason it is useful to be able to view an auction in which you are participating up until it closes. If you are determined to win an auction then some proactive monitoring is required:

If you know that you will not have access to your own computer at the time an auction ends, try to make sure you can get access to the Internet through another computer. This could be done from work, if you are permitted to do this, or from an Internet café.

1. Open the auction page and check how long there is left for the auction. Also check that you are still the high bidder

2. Update the auction page at regular intervals by refreshing your browser. Ideally, this should be done until the final seconds

If you are participating in multiple auctions at the same time, open different windows in your browser so that you can view the auction home pages for each item simultaneously.

3 If you are still the high bidder when the auction closes you will see the following message on the auction page

Payment methods and related issues are looked at in more detail in Chapter Ten.

4 Click here to progress to the payment section

5 You will also be sent an email telling you that you have won the item. Click here to progress to the payment section

Listing items for sale

eBay is a great place to make some extra cash by selling unwanted or unused items that you have lying around the house or hidden in closets or garages. This chapter looks at finding items to sell, preparing them and then opening a seller's account on eBay. It also gives details of how to list items for sale so that you can start an auction as a seller.

Covers

Chapter Six

Deciding what to sell

A lot of eBay users never sell anything on the site, while others use it as a method to raise some extra cash by selling unwanted items that are lying around in lofts and garages. Other people develop this even further and create businesses by selling items on eBay. Whichever group you fall into as a seller, your first task is to decide exactly what you are going to sell. Some areas to look at are:

Just because you think a family heirloom is not worth keeping, this does not mean that all other family members will agree.

- Items that have outgrown their usefulness. Areas to consider are old toys, children's clothes (as long as they are in good condition) and items relating to old hobbies.

- Items that have been replaced by newer products. Electrical goods and computer equipment are frequently being upgraded and there is usually a market for the older models.

- Unwanted presents. Most people have collections of unwanted presents lying around in cupboards and drawers. These can easily be recycled by listing them on eBay.

- Family heirlooms. If you have a family heirloom that you dislike or do not want, it can be sold on eBay (but make sure you are not offending anyone by doing this).

Collections are a very popular area on eBay. If you have a collection, or part of a collection, that you think may be valuable, take it to a professional valuation service or an auction house before you list it on eBay.

- Collections. A lot of people have items that they collected in their childhood and which have since been left to gather dust. On eBay, collections can be one of the most profitable areas for sellers.

Before you start listing items to sell on eBay there are some points to consider:

- Make sure you do not mind parting with particular items and, if required, you have alternatives once you have sold them.

- The items really are yours to sell. Never try to sell anything that you do not own.

- Ask family members if you think anyone may be upset about anything you sell, such as heirlooms.

Sourcing items

The most successful eBay sellers are those who can source items from a variety of locations and keep on finding them. Some areas from which items for sale on eBay can be sourced are:

- Your own house. The closest and probably most prolific source of possible items is within your own home. A quick look through closets and drawers can reveal a number of items that could be put up for auction. When garden sheds, garages and lofts are added there should be a significant, and varied, amount of saleable items.

When selling for someone else make sure that they give you a proper description of the item and details about shipping and packing. Remember, it will be your name that is against the auction.

- From friends and family. As well as selling the goods you find in your own house it is also worthwhile to ask around family and friends to see if they have anything they would like you to sell on their behalf. A lot of people have unwanted items but they are not interested in going to the trouble of actively selling them. If you offer to do this for them, you can then sell the items on eBay. However, make sure that you negotiate a cut of the price for yourself before you start selling.

- Garage sales and jumble sales. Garage sales have grown dramatically in the last decade and traditional jumble sales are still a common feature in church halls and schools around the country. These can be an ideal way to obtain products that can then be resold on eBay. If you are going to do this, haggle to get a good price in order to maximize your profits on eBay.

- Antique shops. If you have a reasonable understanding of antiques then antique shops can be a valuable resource. However, it is vital to make sure that you know how much something is worth when you buy it from an antique shop and that it is genuine. When selling antique items on eBay you will probably be asked a lot of questions by prospective buyers. If possible, try and get a certificate of authentication to provide reassurance for buyers on eBay.

- Live auctions. If you have an eye for a bargain then real auctions could be a good source of items that you can then sell on eBay. If you are participating in a live auction it is important that you find out how much you think an item is worth and set yourself a maximum price for bidding. Ideally, this should be relatively low so that you stand more of a chance of making a profit on eBay. If you are lucky there will be no other bidders and so you may get the item at a bargain price. If there are many bidders and the price is being pushed higher then it may be prudent to stop bidding.

- Small ads. Local newspapers usually carry small ads of items for sale and this can be another profitable area. Always go to see the items that are advertised and check out their condition. Also, always try to haggle the price down. In a lot of cases, people who are selling through the small ads just want to get rid of unwanted items and so they are generally happy to accept less than the advertised price.

When looking to buy items for resale, make sure that there is a market for them – specifically that there are already similar items for sale on eBay. Otherwise you could be left with unsold items.

- Discount shops. Almost all shops occasionally offer items at reduced prices, but some do this more frequently and with greater reductions. Cash and carry stores are ideal for picking up bargains: they frequently have significant discounts on a batch of items (such as televisions) which can then be sold on eBay for a potential profit. If you are looking for these types of bargains you will have to visit the shops fairly regularly as the goods are usually snapped up very quickly.

- End of season sales. Traditional shop sales are also good for picking up cheap items, although a bit of forward thinking is sometimes involved. The trick here is to buy seasonal items at the end of the season and then list them on eBay at the start of the season the following year. For instance, you could buy a batch of discounted swimwear in September and then list it on eBay in March or April the following year.

For more information about trading as a business see Chapter Eleven.

- Wholesalers. Wholesalers usually sell directly to the trade outlets, but if you can persuade one to sell to you then you could have a valuable asset as far as trading on eBay is concerned. If you are dealing with a wholesaler you will probably have to buy large quantities of the items in which you are interested and pay for them promptly.

Preparing items for sale

Traditional retailers spend a lot of time and money ensuring that their goods look their best and are displayed as effectively as possible. This helps to draw in the customers and attract their attention. In a similar way, it is important to prepare your items for sale on eBay as professionally as possible. This will not only help attract buyers but it will also cut down on the possibility of complaints from customers once a sale has been concluded. A little work put in before a sale can save a lot of time and hassle afterwards. Some points to consider when preparing items for sale:

eBayers are generally very accommodating but they can be highly critical of inaccurate or misleading descriptions of items.

- Make sure the product matches the description used on eBay. This is essential, as it is an area that can result in negative feedback from disgruntled buyers. If you know there is a defect in an item then say so in the description. The buyer will find out anyway once they receive the item, so it is better to be honest at the outset. When you are preparing the item, be overly critical yourself to see if you can spot any defects or faults in the item that should be listed. Once you have prepared the item, note down a draft description and then check that it is an accurate reflection of the item.

- Ensure that items are clean and respectable. This is essential for items such as second-hand clothes, which have to be cleaned before they are listed on eBay. Even with other items it is important to make sure they are as clean as possible, even if this just means rubbing a damp cloth over something. With some items it is impossible to clean them completely, in which case this information should be included in the description.

If you are selling new items, try to make sure they are in their original packaging. This acts as an added guarantee of their condition.

- Make sure the item is working. For items such as electrical products or computer equipment, it is the seller's responsibility to make sure that the items are working properly when they are posted. Test items as thoroughly as possible; for example, if you are selling a television and video recorder in one auction, make sure they work individually and together.

- Take a photograph of the item, for inclusion on the site, after it has been prepared and is looking its best.

Researching similar items

A bit of research is just as important for selling as for buying items. This gives you an idea of how much similar items have sold for, the condition they were in, the amount of shipping charged and the number of bidders. Once you have this information it can be used to help determine the listing for your own items. The best way to research similar items from a seller's point of view is to look at completed auctions for these products. To do this:

1 Open the Advanced Search page and enter the name of the item for sale. Check on the Completed Listings Only box

Searching for items from completed auctions gives you an idea of the price they actually fetched, rather than a price mid-way through a particular auction.

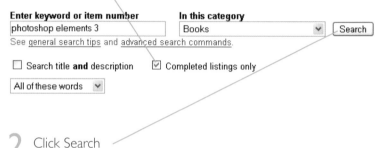

2 Click Search

3 A list of similar items is displayed in the search results. Click on one to view its details

4 View the description and the photograph of the item to get an idea of its condition. This can then be compared with the price it fetched, which can be viewed on the search results page

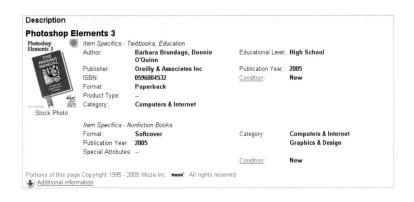

5 Check the shipping and payment details. This gives you an idea of how much to charge for shipping and the amount of flexibility that other sellers are offering

The more payment options there are, the better it is for the buyer.

Shipping, payment details and return policy

Shipping Cost	Services Available	Available to
US $3.50	US Postal Service Media Mail™	United States Only

Will ship to United States.

Shipping insurance
US $1.30 Optional

Seller's payment instructions
Will only accept cashiers checks and money orders. Will only ship within the

Payment methods accepted

• Money order/Cashiers check
Learn about payment methods.

Accessing the seller's account page

The first step in becoming a seller on eBay is to set up a seller's account. This is obligatory as it provides eBay with the means to deduct the fees that are payable for every sale. To set up a seller's account:

1 Log in and click here

It is better to participate in a few auctions as a buyer before you start selling items. This will give you a feel for how eBay works and the types of things that happen in an auction.

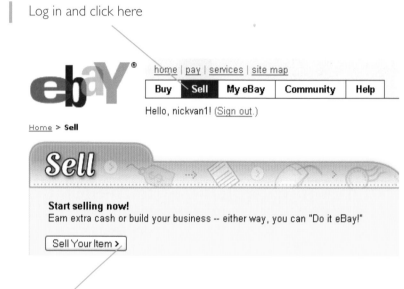

2 Click here to start the selling process

3 Scroll down the page to find links to more information about selling items on eBay:

How do you sell on eBay?

Prepare	List	Get Paid
Decide what you want to sell, then research similar items that have sold on eBay.	Describe your item with details like brand and condition, take a photo, then list your item in a few easy steps.	After your listing ends successfully, you can receive payment immediately with PayPal--it's simple!

Selling Resources

Getting Started
Selling Overview | Learning Center
How to Sell Tour | The Perfect Listing
Accepting Online Payments | See all...

Seller Community
Seller Discussion Board
Answer Center | Security Center
Seller Groups | Giving Works | See all...

Best Practices
Research NEW! | Pricing | Selling Formats
Merchandising | Promotional Tools
Packing & Shipping | See all...

Selling Solutions
Individual | Small Business
Enterprise | Selling on eBay motors
Trading Assistant Program | See all...

See advanced selling resources...

Creating a seller's account

To set up a seller's account to start selling items:

1 Make sure you have your credit or debit card and bank account details to hand. These are used to verify your identification and also for the basis of the account itself

Seller's Account: Verify Information

1 Verify Information   2. Provide Identification   3. Select How to Pay Seller Fees

Please have the following ready, as you'll need both to sell on eBay:
- Credit or debit card

- Check book (bank account)

eBay has strict rules about how they use personal details and they are committed to not passing them on to any third party that does not require them.

2 Enter your personal details. Although you have already entered these when you initially registered on eBay, they have to be entered again when you want to become a seller

First, verify that your information below is correct.

First name
Nick

Last name
Vandome

Street address
Main Street

City
Boston

State / Province
Massachusetts

Zip / Postal code
MA 01720

Country
United States

Primary telephone
(1234) 567 - 891   ext.:

Continue >

3 Click Continue to move through the steps to complete the process for setting up the seller's account

Listing items to sell

Once you have created a seller's account you can then start listing items to sell. The process is begun in the same way as shown on page 98 for initially setting up a seller's account. Then an item can be listed for sale as follows:

1 Select this button to list the item for sale in an auction

If you do not want to sell your item in an auction, check on the Sell at a Fixed Price button. This will make your listing a Buy It Now sale only.

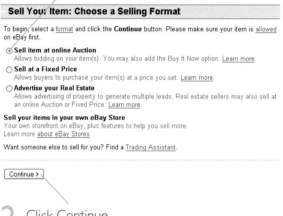

2 Click Continue

3 Click here to select a main category for the item. This is the category under which it will appear in the eBay categories listings

Try not to use the Everything Else category, as it is a bit vague when people are searching for items. There are enough eBay categories that you should be able to find one to match the item you are selling.

4 If the item does not seem to fit into any of the main categories, select the Everything Else option at the bottom of the page

⊙ Everything Else   Gifts & Occasions, Genealogy, Weird Stuff and More!

5 Alternatively, enter a description of the item here and click Search

6 A category listing is pre-selected, based on the information entered in the search box

If you do not search for a category using the Search box, you will be able to select a sub-category for your item after you have selected a main category.

7 Click Continue

Writing a description

One of the most important elements in a listing to sell an item is the description. This tells prospective buyers about the item, the condition it is in and any additional information you want to disclose. To add a description of an item:

The item title appears in the search results page.

1 Enter the title here. This should state exactly what the item is

Sell Your Item: Describe Your Item

1. Category   **2** **Title & Description**   3. Pictures & Details   4. Payment & Shipping

Item title *Required

Photoshop Elements 3

35 characters left; no HTML, asterisks, or quotes.
Include specific details about your item. Get tips on writing a good title. Learn More

Subtitle ($0.50)

2 Click here and select whether the item is new or used and its format, if applicable

Condition

Used ▾

Format

Softcover ▾

Publication Year

2005

Be as honest as possible when writing descriptions. In the long-term, you will gain little or no advantage by not describing items accurately.

3 Enter a detailed, comprehensive description of the item. Include details of any faults or defects

Item description *

Describe your items features, benefits, and condition. Be sure to include in your d dimensions or size. You may also want to include notable markings or signatures Books.

General level book on Photoshop Elements 3. Covering all aspects of the program, including image editing, sharing, organizing and creating. Fully illustrated in color with comprehensive step-by-step details for each feature and technique. The book is the US version and in mint condition.

Enter <p> to start a new paragraph. Get more HTML tips.

Spell check | Preview description

4 Click Continue to move to the next step

Note: After you click **Continue**, you may be asked to download a small file. This page does not appear, change your picture selection method.

‹ Back   Continue ›

Pictures, price and auction duration

The next stage of the process is to add images to accompany the description of the item, determine the starting price for the item and set the duration of the auction. To do this:

The starting price is the price at which the auction for an item will begin. This is the minimum price that a buyer has to initially bid for an item.

1 Enter the starting price here

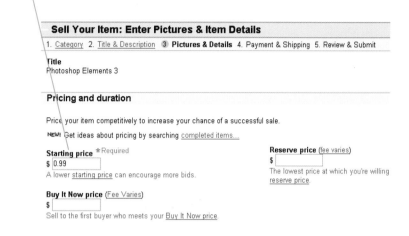

Sell Your Item: Enter Pictures & Item Details

1. Category 2. Title & Description ③ **Pictures & Details** 4. Payment & Shipping 5. Review & Submit

Title
Photoshop Elements 3

Pricing and duration

Price your item competitively to increase your chance of a successful sale.

NEW! Get ideas about pricing by searching completed items...

Starting price *Required
$ 0.99
A lower starting price can encourage more bids.

Reserve price (fee varies)
$
The lowest price at which you're willing reserve price.

Buy It Now price (Fee Varies)
$
Sell to the first buyer who meets your Buy It Now price.

Be careful about setting a starting price that is artificially low in the hope of attracting a lot of bidders. If you only get one bid at the starting price then this is the amount you will have to sell the item for (unless you also set a reserve, as explained on page 114).

2 Click here and select the duration for the auction. The minimum is 1 day and maximum is 10 days

Duration *
5 days ▼
When to use a 1-day duration.

3 Select this option to have the auction start as soon as the item is submitted for listing

Start time

⦿ Start listing when submitted
◯ Schedule start time ($0.10) Select a date... ▼   Select a time... ▼ PDT

Try to ensure that your auction goes over at least one weekend, when there are likely to be more people with time to look at eBay.

4 Select this option to select a specific time for the start of the auction. This gives you more control over when an auction starts and, more importantly, when it finishes

If possible, make sure the ending time for an auction is when you will be able to access eBay. This way you will be able to contact the winning bidder immediately.

To list multiple items in a single auction, also known as a Dutch auction, you must have your direct debit details on file, or have an overall feedback rating of 20 or higher, or if you have a PayPal account and an overall feedback rating of 10 or higher.

5 Scroll down the page and select the quantity for the item you have for sale. The default is one, but if you have several identical items to sell, click the Multiple Item link (if you are eligible)

Quantity *

| Individual Items | Lots |

**Quantity *
1

Learn more about <u>multiple item</u> listings.

6 Enter the location of the item

Item location

ZIP Code: Not specified
Location display: Perth, United Kingdom
<u>Change</u>

7 Click here to select an image to accompany the item's description

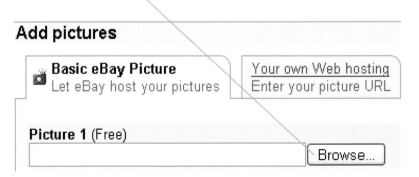

Add pictures

Basic eBay Picture
Let eBay host your pictures

<u>Your own Web hosting</u>
Enter your picture URL

Picture 1 (Free)

Browse...

8 Browse your hard drive, select an image and click Open (Windows) or Choose (Mac)

You can add an image from an existing website of your own, if you have one. To do this, click on the Your Own Web Hosting link and enter the full URL (Web address). Make sure this is for the image (with a .jpg, .gif, or .png extension) rather than a Web page (with an .htm extension).

It is strictly prohibited to link to images on other people's websites, unless you get their permission.

9 The selected image is noted here. This will appear next to the description of the item on the auction page

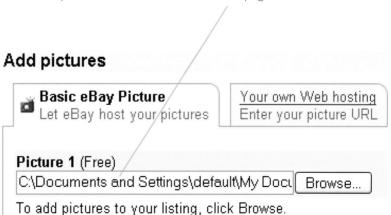

Add pictures

Basic eBay Picture
Let eBay host your pictures

Your own Web hosting
Enter your picture URL

Picture 1 (Free)

C:\Documents and Settings\default\My Docu   Browse...

To add pictures to your listing, click Browse.

Enhanced options

eBay offers a number of enhanced options to make a listing stand out more from the crowd. To use the enhanced options:

1 Tick this boxes to have your listing displayed more prominently at a larger size

To use the Supersize option the source images have to be a minimum of 500 by 500 pixels. Otherwise this option cannot be used.

Picture options
Applies to all pictures.
◉ Standard
Standard pictures will appear within a 400- by 400- pixel area.
☐ Supersize Pictures ($0.75)
Extra large pictures will appear within a 500- by 500- pixel area, or up to 800- by 800- pixel area, if your pictures are larger.
☐ **NEW!** Picture Show ($0.25)
Multiple pictures will appear in a slideshow player at the top of the item page.
◯ Picture Pack ($1.00 for up to 6 pictures or $1.50 for 7 to 12 pictures)
Get Gallery, Supersize, Picture Show and additional pictures for maximum exposure. Save up to $1.50!

2 Click here to have all of the picture options applied to your listing

3 Click here to select a theme for how the listing is displayed

The more enhanced options that are selected, the greater the overall cost.

Listing designer

Listing designer ($0.10)
Get both a theme and layout to complement your listing.

Select a theme
Category Specific (67) ▼

Baby-Rattle
Boats
Books and Music
Books-Border
Books-Stacks
Business and Industrial-Steel
Casino
Clothing and Accessories-Men
Clothing and Accessories-Modern

Select a layout
Standard
Photo on the left
Photo on the right
Photo on the bottom
Photo on the top

Preview listing

...cont'd

4 Click here to have your listing appear in bold

☑ Bold ($1.00)
   Attract buyers' attention and set your listing apart - use **Bold**. See example
☑ Border ($3.00)
   Get noticed - outline your listing with an eye-catching frame. See example
☑ Highlight ($5.00)
   Make your listing stand out with a colored band in Search results. See example

Emphasizing items is looked at in more detail in Chapter Seven.

5 Click here to have your listing appear with a colored band behind it to make it stand out more

6 Click here to add a border around your listing

☑ Bold ($1.00)
   Attract buyers' attention and set your listing apart - use **Bold**. See example
☑ Border ($3.00)
   Get noticed - outline your listing with an eye-catching frame. See example
☑ Highlight ($5.00)
   Make your listing stand out with a colored band in Search results. See example

Including a page counter is always worthwhile as it is free and it gives you an idea about the level of interest your auction is generating.

7 If you want a page counter with your listing, select one of the options here. This will show how many visitors you have had to your listing once the auction starts

Page counter
○ No counter
○ Andale Style
◉ Green LED
○ Thanks for looking!   Hidden (Only you see page views)

[‹ Back] [Continue ›]

8 Click Continue to move to the next step of the listing process

Payment and shipping

Any buyer should pay careful attention to the amount of shipping and the methods of delivery. Therefore it is important for the seller to give some thought to these and to try to make the entire listing as attractive as possible to any prospective buyers. To enter the payment and shipping details:

Don't make shipping prohibitively expensive or try to subsidize a low starting price for an item by increasing the shipping cost. This practice is not allowed by eBay.

1 Tick this box if you want buyers to have the option of using PayPal to pay for an item

Payment methods

Choose the payment methods you'll accept from buyers.

PayPal is a means of transferring money electronically between buyers and sellers, and is the most commonly used method of payment on eBay.

PayPal

MasterCard VISA AMEX DISCOVER eCHECK

PayPal allows you to accept credit card payments in multiple currencies from buyers in 45 countries worldwide.

☑ PayPal payment notification will go to: nickvandome@hotmail.com   Edit preferences
PayPal fees may apply.

2 Tick the other payment options which you are willing to accept

Never accept cash as a means of payment, even if it is suggested by the buyer.

Other payment methods
☑ Money Order / Cashier's Check

☑ Personal Check

☐ Other / See Item Description

Merchant credit cards
Only for sellers accepting credit card purchases through their own merchant account.
☑ Visa/MasterCard   ☐ Discover   ☐ American Express

For a more detailed look at payment options see Chapter Ten.

3 Select an option for where you are willing to send the item

Even if you state that you are only willing to ship items to one location you may still have people from around the world bidding on your auction.

Ship-to locations ＊Required

◉ Will ship to the United States and the following (check all that apply):
Reach more buyers - learn more about shipping internationally.

- ☑ Worldwide
- ☐ Americas
- ☐ Europe
- ☐ Asia
- ☐ Canada
- ☑ United Kingdom
- ☐ Australia
- ☐ Mexico
- ☐ Germany
- ☐ Japan

◯ Will not ship - local pickup only
Specify pickup arrangements in the Payment Instructions box below.

4 Click here for shipping options

Domestic Shipping (offer up to 3 services)

US Postal Service Priority Mail ▾

Select a shipping service
US Postal Service Priority Mail
US Postal Service Express Mail
US Postal Service Parcel Post
US Postal Service Media Mail
US Postal Service First Class Mail
UPS Ground
UPS 3 Day Select
UPS 2nd Day Air
UPS Next Day Air Saver
UPS Next Day Air
Standard Flat Rate Shipping Service
Expedited shipping service
Other (see description)
Local Delivery/Pickup

Try to have more than one option for the method of shipping. This will allow the buyer to select a cheaper option if they want.

5 Select a method of shipping

Shipping & sales tax ＊

Specify a flat cost for each shipping service you offer, or have costs address. Learn more about specifying shipping costs.

Flat: same cost to all buyers	**Calculated:** based on buyer's address

Domestic Shipping (offer up to 3 services)

US Postal Service Priority Mail ▾ $ 3.00

Add service | Remove service and have buyers contact me later

6 Enter an amount for shipping

If you are in any doubt about the amount of shipping to charge, take the item to the post office, get it weighed and find out exactly how much it is for different shipping services.

International Shipping (offer up to 3 services)

Standard Int'l Flat Rate Shipping ▾ $ 4.00

To: ☑ Worldwide ☐ Americas ☐ Europe ☐ Asia
☐ Canada ☑ United ☐ Australia
☐ Mexico Kingdom ☐ Japan
☐ Germany

Add service | Remove service

7 Click here to select another shipping option. This can be set in the same way as the first one

Some sellers add a small amount to the actual cost of shipping to cover their time spent packaging and posting it.

8 Enter details about a return policy for the item

Return policy

☑ **Returns Accepted** - Specify a return policy. Learn More.

Item must be returned within 30 Days ▾

Refund will be given as Money Back ▾

Return Policy Details

No hassle return policy within 30 days of receipt.

If you include shipping insurance this will be an additional charge to cover insurance for the item if it is lost or damaged while in transit. This is most frequently used when sending items abroad.

9 Enter specific payment instructions

Having a transparent and robust return policy is a good way of making buyers feel confident about doing business with you.

Payment instructions

Give clear instructions to assist your buyer with payment and shipping.

Increase sales by offering a shipping discount in your description for multiple item purchases.

Please send payment within 14 days after safe receipt of goods.

Reviewing a listing

At the end of the listing process it is possible to review all of the details you have entered for the item you are selling:

1   Review the title, description and images used. Try to look at these with fresh eyes and imagine how prospective buyers will view these details

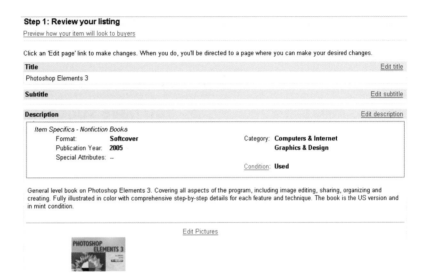

2   Scroll down the page and review the fees you will be charged once the listing is submitted

The Insertion Fee is based on the starting price that you have specified for an item. It is non-refundable even if your item does not sell. For more information on eBay fees, see Chapter Ten.

Step 2: Review the fees and submit your listing

Listing fees	
Insertion fee:	**$ 0.25**
Total added listing fees:	**$ 0.25**

3 If you are happy with the
details of the item, click
Submit Listing. If you want
to make changes click Back

< Back   Submit Listing

4 Once you have submitted your listing you will see the following
confirmation message:

Sell Your Item: Congratulations

 You have successfully listed your item

View your listing: <u>Photoshop Elements 3</u>

<u>Track this item</u> in My eBay

Sell a Similar Item or <u>Sell a Different Item</u>

5 Your listing will also appear on the Items I'm Selling section on
your My eBay page

6 You will also be sent an email confirming your listing:

Your Listing Has Been Confirmed

Dear nickvan1,
Your item has been successfully listed on eBay. It may take several hours for your listing to appear in
eBay search results.

Listing details

Item name:	Photoshop Elements 3
Item number:	
Listing format:	Auction
Main category:	Books:Nonfiction Books
Quantity:	1
Start price:	US $0.99
Listing duration:	5 days
Start date:	25-May-05 15:36:38 BST
End date:	30-May-05 15:36:38 BST

Advanced listing

This chapter looks at how to create a listing to give an item the best possible chance of selling and obtaining a good price. It covers capturing the best images possible, using HTML to improve text formatting and giving your listings more prominence when other eBayers search for similar items. It also has details of creating an About Me page, which is your own self-promotion Web page on eBay.

Covers

Chapter Seven

To reserve or not to reserve

One of the decisions that you will have to make when listing an item for sale is whether to include a reserve price. This is a minimum price at which you are prepared to sell the item: once the auction is completed you do not have to sell the item if the reserve price has not been met. Buyers can see that there is a reserve price attached to an item, but not how much it is. There is no minimum value for a reserve price. The advantage of a reserve price is:

● You are guaranteed a minimum amount for an item; if this is not met, you do not have to sell the item.

The disadvantage of a reserve price is:

● It can put off buyers; since they cannot see the amount of the reserve price, they are unsure of how much they have to bid just to meet the reserve, never mind to win the auction.

When a reserve is set for an item, a starting price for the auction is also listed. This is usually significantly lower than the reserve price: the idea is that bidders will be attracted by the low starting price and the bidding will go above the reserve. In practice it is usually better to have no reserve and a higher starting price. Until the reserve price is met, there is a note underneath the item stating "Reserve Not Met". The reserve price is entered during the listing process.

If you set a reserve price for an item, this will be the figure upon which the insertion fee will be calculated, not the starting price.

To add a reserve price to an item for sale:

1 Enter a starting price for the auction

Starting price ✱Required

$ 10.00

A lower <u>starting price</u> can encourage more bids.

2 Enter the reserve price: the minimum amount which you are prepared to accept for the item

Reserve price (fee varies)

$ 50.00

Capturing images

No matter how good a textual description of an item is, a good picture can make the difference between a successful, profitable sale and an auction with no bidders at all. There is a lot of competition on eBay so everything that you can do to give yourself an advantage is important.

When capturing images for use in an auction, there are some points that you should follow to get the best possible initial image:

If you are not a confident photographer, enlist the help of a family member or a friend who is more proficient with a camera, and ask them to take some pictures of your item.

- Get as close to the object as possible. Buyers want to see the object itself, not the background or the surrounding area.

- Make sure the background is as neutral as possible and does not detract from the item itself. For instance, do not take pictures of items against heavily patterned carpets.

- Make sure that images are in focus. If you find an image is out of focus, take another one. A bit of effort at this stage could pay dividends when the item is up for auction.

Use a tripod if possible, to make sure the picture is composed properly and that the image is in focus and does not suffer from camera shake.

- Capture the item at different angles. You can include up to a dozen images with a listing (at a cost of $0.15 each after the first one) so make the most of this and include shots from the front, back, top and side, if applicable. You may not use all of the images but it is good to have a choice.

- Use natural light if possible. The best lighting for taking photographs occurs either first thing in the morning or just before dusk. This produces a natural, soft light that is ideal for photography. If you cannot manage this, then still try and take images in daylight. If you have to take them inside then use a flash, but make sure there is no glare reflected off the subject. This can be a particular problem with glass objects.

- If you are using a digital camera, use a low resolution setting, such as 640 x 480. This will not affect the quality of the image when it is used on eBay, but it will create a smaller file size, which will speed up the downloading time. Similarly, if you are scanning a hard-copy image, use a low resolution.

Sample images

1 This is a poor image because the subject is too small, is slightly obscured and the background is too dark (there is not enough contrast between the subject and the background)

2 This is a better composition because the subject takes up more of the image and the back is more neutral so it does not distract from the subject. However, it is slightly out of focus which spoils the overall effect

3 This is the type of image that should be used to accompany a listing. It is sharp and crisp and the subject is prominently displayed

Editing images

The example screen shots in this chapter use Photoshop Elements, but similar features exist in the other image editing programs.

Even if you capture an excellent initial image, it will probably benefit from some digital editing in an image editing program such as Photoshop, Photoshop Elements, Paint Shop Pro or Ulead Express. Even some basic techniques can produce dramatic results.

Editing Levels

A pixel (which is a contraction of "picture element") is a colored dot in a digital image. Most images are made up of thousands, or millions, of pixels.

The levels in a digital image determine the distribution of the lightest and darkest pixels in the image, spread across a graph known as a histogram. If there are not enough pixels at the extremes of white and black, the image can appear either over- or under-exposed. If this happens, the Levels command in a digital image editing program can be used to redistribute the pixels so that there are some at both extremes of the graph. This has the result of improving the overall tone of the image. In some programs this can be done with an Auto Levels command, but it can also be done manually. To do this:

Never use image editing software to change the physical appearance of an item you are selling. This is dishonest and could result in problems once the sale has been completed. Only use image editing software to enhance what is already in the picture.

Open an image and access the Levels dialog window

For a detailed look at digital photography and digital imaging, have a look at "Digital Photography in Easy Steps".

2 The tonal range of pixels in the image is shown here. If there are gaps at either end it means the image is either too dark or too light at the extremes of this graph

3 Drag these sliders to improve the tonal range of the image

Most image editing programs have an Auto Levels option which will adjust the level automatically. This is worth trying, but, generally, the results are not as accurate as doing it manually.

4 An image before Levels correction has been applied. It generally looks a bit "flat" with a limited tonal range

5 Once Levels correction has been applied, the image has a much better tonal range and the main subject stands out more

Brightness and Contrast

Another simple improvement to an image can be made by adjusting the brightness and contrast. To do this:

1 Open an image that looks either too dull or too bright

2 Access the Brightness/ Contrast dialog window and drag these sliders

Tick the Preview box to see the changes take effect as they are made in the dialog box.

3 The final image now looks much brighter and sharper

Sharpening

Sharpening is a technique that improves the clarity of an image. Although it can be used to try to make an out of focus image a bit clearer, it is most effective on a standard digital image that appears in reasonable focus. A lot of digital cameras apply some sharpening to images as they are captured and if this is also done in an image editing program it can give an already acceptable image added clarity. To apply sharpening:

 Sharpening works by increasing the contrast between the edges of adjoining pixels in an image. This creates a greater definition between pixels, resulting in a sharper image.

1 Open an image that is acceptable but either slightly blurry or marginally out of focus

 In addition to the standard sharpening option, there are additional options for applying greater degrees of sharpening. These are Sharpen More, Sharpen Edges and Unsharp Mask.

2 Select the Sharpening option (usually found under the Filter menu in image editing programs)

3 The image appears clearer and more sharply defined

Optimizing images

Optimization is a term given to the technique of making image files as small as possible, while still retaining a suitable quality. This is important for images that are used on the Web because the larger the file size, the longer it takes for them to download. Also, most consumer digital cameras are now capable of taking large images, in terms of both file size and physical dimensions. This is excellent for printing, but unnecessary for the Web since the files will be viewed at sizes and resolutions that are far smaller than in the original image. Although eBay does not stipulate that images have to be under a certain file size when they are sent for inclusion with a listing, it is a good idea to try to make them as small as possible. This is done by changing the physical size of the image by removing unwanted pixels. To do this:

Tick the Resample Image box to enable the size of the image to be changed. Tick the Constrain Proportions box to change the size of the image proportionally.

Make sure the image is big enough for any picture options that have been selected in eBay: a standard picture appears in an area of 400 x 400 pixels, while a supersize picture appears in an area of 500 x 500 pixels. Do not reduce the image size beyond these dimensions.

1 Open the Image Size dialog window. The current dimensions are shown here. Tick the Constrain Proportions and Resample Image boxes

2 Enter a new figure for the Width, and the height will be adjusted proportionally. This will also reduce the file size of the image. Click OK to apply the changes

Using HTML

HyperText Markup Language (HTML) is a markup code which is used to format the vast majority of the pages on the Web. It is not a full-blown programming language but rather a way of displaying information. It uses tags to instruct Web browsers how certain items on the page should be displayed. These tags are contained within angled brackets and there are usually, but not always, an opening and a closing tag. So if you want to produce bold text on a Web page you could use:

<b>Welcome to my Web page</b>

When adding descriptions of items in an eBay listing it is possible to use HTML code to make the text look more interesting and stand out more. There are a number of simple HTML tags that can be added within the description box of an eBay listing:

If you are familiar with HTML you can include your own markup for an item description. This will show up once the item is listed.

Bold

| Add a <b></b> opening and closing tag to create bold

```
<b>Main heading</b>
```

Enter <p> to start a new paragraph. Get more <u>HTML tips</u>.

Spell check | Preview description

For more information about HTML, see "HTML in Easy Steps".

2 Click Preview Description to see how the effect will look

http://pages.ebay.com - View your description...

Main heading

Close Window

Done

Italics

1 Add an <i></i> opening and closing tag to create italics

`<i>Main heading</i>`

Enter <p> to start a new paragraph. Get more HTML tips.

Spell check | Preview description

Don't use underlining in HTML as this could be mistaken for a hyperlink once it is displayed on an eBay Web page.

2 Click Preview Description to see how the effect will look

http://pages.ebay.com - View your description ...

Main heading

[Close Window]

Done

Main heading

1 Add an <h1> </h1> opening and closing tag to create a main heading

`<h1>Main heading</h1>`

Enter <p> to start a new paragraph. Get more HTML tips.

Spell check | Preview description

2 Click Preview Description to see how the effect will look

http://pages.ebay.com - View your description - ...

Main heading

[Close Window]

Done

Sub heading

There are six levels of headings within HTML.

1 Add an <h2> </h2> opening and closing tag to create a sub heading

```
<h1>Main heading</h1>
<h2>Sub heading</h2>
```

Enter <p> to start a new paragraph. Get more HTML tips.

Spell check | Preview description

2 Click Preview Description to see how the effect will look

New paragraph

A single line break can be created by including the <br> tag. This does not have a corresponding closing tag.

1 Add a <p></p> opening and closing tag to create a new paragraph

```
<h1>Main heading</h1>
<h2>Sub heading</h2>
<p>Main content goes here</p>
```

Enter <p> to start a new paragraph. Get more HTML tips.

Spell check | Preview description

2 Click Preview Description to see how the effect will look

Font color

1 Add a
<font color>
</font> opening and
closing tag to create a
text color

```
<h1>Main heading</h1>
<h2>Sub heading</h2>
<p><font color=green>Main content goes
here</font></p>
```

Enter <p> to start a new paragraph. Get more HTML tips.

Spell check | Preview description

The <font> tag can have different attributes applied to it, such as face (for a different font), size and color. For each of these the attribute has to have a property assigned to it, for example <font size=4>.

2 Click Preview
Description to see
how the effect will
look

Font size

1 Add a
<font size>
</font> opening and
closing tag to create a
text size

```
<h1>Main heading</h1>
<h2>Sub heading</h2>
<p><font size=5>Main content goes here</font></p>
```

Enter <p> to start a new paragraph. Get more HTML tips.

Spell check | Preview description

2 Click Preview
Description to see
how the effect will
look

Size and color

The <font size> tag and attribute can be used to create text that is larger than the <h1> tag, which appears at a preset size.

1 Add a combination of font tags to change the size and color of text

```
<h1>Main heading</h1>
<h2>Sub heading</h2>
<p><font size=5 color=red>Main content goes
here</font></p>
```

Enter <p> to start a new paragraph. Get more HTML tips.

Spell check | Preview description

2 Click Preview Description to see how the effect will look

Center

1 Add a   opening and closing tag to center text

```
<h1>Main heading</h1>
<h2>Sub heading</h2>
<p><font size=5 color=red><center>Main content goes
here</center></font></p>
```

Enter <p> to start a new paragraph. Get more HTML tips.

Spell check | Preview description

2 Click Preview Description to see how the effect will look

Bulleted list

The code for a bulleted list consists of the <ul> tag (which stands for Unordered List), and the <li> tag (which stands for List Item) for each bullet point.

1 Add <ul><li> </li></ul> opening and closing tags to create a bulleted list

```
<h1>Main heading</h1>
<h2>Sub heading</h2>
<p><font size=5 color=red><center>Main content goes
here</center></font></p>
<ul>
<li>List item 1</li>
<li>List item 2</li>
<li>List item 3</li>
</ul>
```

Enter <p> to start a new paragraph. Get more HTML tips.

Spell check | Preview description

2 Click Preview Description to see how the effect will look

Numbered list

The code for a numbered list consists of the <ol> tag (which stands for Ordered List), and the <li> tag for each numbered item.

1 Add <ol><li> </li></ol> opening and closing tags to create a numbered list

```
<h1>Main heading</h1>
<h2>Sub heading</h2>
<p><font size=5 color=red><center>Main content goes
here</center></font></p>
<ol>
<li>List item 1</li>
<li>List item 2</li>
<li>List item 3</li>
</ol>
```

Enter <p> to start a new paragraph. Get more HTML tips.

Spell check | Preview description

2 Click Preview Description to see how the effect will look

Horizontal rule

1 Add an <hr> tag to create a horizontal rule

```
<h1>Main heading</h1>
<h2>Sub heading</h2>
<p><font size=5 color=red><center>Main content goes
here</center></font></p>
<hr>
<ol>
<li>List item 1</li>
<li>List item 2</li>
<li>List item 3</li>
</ol>
```

Enter <p> to start a new paragraph. Get more HTML tips.

Spell check | Preview description

2 Click Preview Description to see how the effect will look

Tables

1 Add <table> <tr><td></td> </tr></table> tags to create a table

```
<h1>Main heading</h1>
<h2>Sub heading</h2>
<p><font size=5 color=red><center>Main content goes
here</center></font></p>
<table border=1 width=100%>
<tr><td>One</td><td>Two</td></tr>
<tr><td>Three</td><td>Four</td></tr>
</table>
```

Enter <p> to start a new paragraph. Get more HTML tips.

Spell check | Preview description

2 Click Preview Description to see how the effect will look

About Me page

The About Me page is an opportunity to go in for a bit of self-promotion within eBay. It is your own personal Web page that you can use to tell other eBayers a bit about yourself, your hobbies and the types of items that you like buying and selling. All registered eBay users can create their own About Me page and it is free to do so. Once you have created an About Me page a new icon appears next to your user ID. To create an About Me page:

The information on the About Me page should be as relevant as possible to your eBay activities.

1 Access the About Me authoring page either from the People section of the Community site or via the About Me link in the eBay sitemap, which can be accessed from the main navigation bar

More Community Programs

- **eBay Giving Works**
  Buy and sell on eBay for charity—do well by doing good.
- **Refer a Friend**
  Introduce your friends to eBay and earn up to 5,000 Anything Points per month.
- **Create an About Me page**
  Express yourself and build trust with this personalized page.

A-Z Index of Help Topics

A B C D E F G H I J K L M N
O P Q R S T U V W-Z ALL

About Me
About Me Guidelines (Policy)
About Me HTML Tags
About Me Pages

2 The About Me introduction page explains a bit more about what the page does and the advantages of having one. Click here to continue

About Me

Tell the world about you and your interests

- **Talk about who you are**
  You'll soon find other people with similar interests in eBay's community
- **Describe your collecting or selling passions**
  Relate how you began collecting for fun or selling for profit
- **Build trust and confidence among potential trading partners**
  Highlight your trading record to reassure potential buyers or sellers
- **Get your own personalized eBay page with the me icon**
  Send others to http://members.ebay.com/aboutme/nickvan1/

Create your About Me page

Begin by clicking the button below.

[Create Your Page]

3 Click here to use the About Me wizard to create the page. Click Continue

About Me : Choose Page Creation Option

1 Choose Page Creation Option   2. Enter Page Content   3. Preview and Submit

How would you like to create your page?

◉ **Use our easy Step-by-Step process**

○ **Enter your own HTML code**

[‹ Back]   [Continue ›]

4 Enter a page title and any information about yourself that you
want to appear on the About Me page

In order to include
an image on
your About Me
page you have to
have one already
hosted on another website.

5 Enter a URL for any images you want to include on the page and
give the picture a title

6 Select whether you want your feedback displayed on your page
and select any website links you want included

If you have any
negative feedback
it is not a good
idea to have this
displayed on your
About Me page.

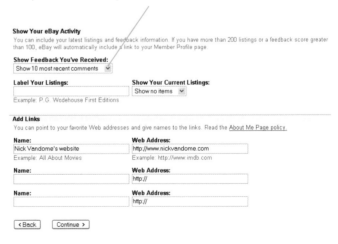

7 Select a format for your page and scroll down the page to preview it

About Me: Preview and Submit

1. Choose Page Creation Option   2. Enter Page Content   ③ **Preview and Submit**

Select a page layout from the three shown here (Layout B is shown below).

○ **Layout "A"**   ◉ **Layout "B"**

Once you've chosen a layout that you like, click the **Submit** button below.

Note: If you don't have JavaScript enabled on your computer, you'll still be able to choose any of these layouts. However, you won't be able to preview your selection below.

[‹ Back]   [Submit ›]

8 Preview the page and, if you are happy with it, click Submit to have your About Me page uploaded onto eBay

The Preview page may look slightly different from the final published page, particularly some of the font sizes.

About Me: **nickvan1** (15 ☆)

Nick Vandome's About Me on eBay page

Welcome to my About Me page. I work with computers and sell mainly electronic equipment. I also buy camping equipment, squash equipment and used books.

Favorite Links

Nick Vandome's website

Feedbacks

User:	Date:May-25-05
03:17:32 PDT	
Praise: Great buyer...prompt payment, valued customer, highly recommended.	

User:	Date:Oct-31-04
11:28:30 PST	
Praise: Item delivered speedily and in good condition. Good contact too.	

9 A confirmation message appears stating that your About Me page has been created. Click here to view the page on eBay as other users will see it

Your about me page has been edited

Your new About Me page has been successfully created. You should shortly be able to view it at this Web address: http://members.ebay.com/aboutme/nickvan1.

Where would you like to go next?
* Item I last looked at
* My eBay
* More Community Resources

10 Preview the live About Me page

About Me: nickvan1 (15 ☆) me   Edit | Delete

Nick Vandome's About Me on eBay page

Welcome to my About Me page. I work with computers and sell mainly electronic equipment. I also buy camping equipment, squash equipment and used books.

Favorite Links

Feedbacks

User:
Date: May-25-05 03:17:32 PDT
Praise: Great buyer...prompt payment, valued customer, highly recommended.

User:

Have a look at the About Me pages of other eBay users to see what they have to say about themselves, and the style of their pages.

11 Once you have created an About Me page, a new icon appears next to your User ID. This applies to all users who have created their own About Me page

Seller information

nickvan1 (15 ☆) me

Feedback Score: 15
Positive Feedback: 100%
Member since Aug-11-04 in United Kingdom

Read feedback comments

Add to Favorite Sellers

Ask seller a question

View seller's other items

Safe Buying Tips

Emphasizing items

When listing items for sale you can boost your chances of a successful sale by emphasizing your item with either bold or a highlighted background. There is a small additional listing fee for this, but it can be a worthwhile investment.

Adding bold

To add bold to a listing:

1. On the listing page, tick this box

   ☑ Bold ($1.00)
   Attract buyers' attention and set your listing apart - use **Bold**.

2. Once the item is listed, the text appears in bold to make it stand out more next to other listings

   ☐ **$648 9NWT WOMEN PIQUE PERU LACOSTE SHIRTS POLO 36/4 S**
   10 GORGEOUS COLORS MONEY BACK GUARANTEE FAST SHIPPING!

   ☐ **NWT Gap Maternity CLOTHES Pants & Shirts SIZE 10 MEDIUM**

Adding highlights

To add a highlighted background to a listing:

1. On the listing page, tick this box

   ☑ Highlight ($5.00)
   Make your listing stand out with a colored band in Search results.

2. The whole listing appears on a colored background

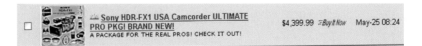

   ☐ **Sony HDR-FX1 USA Camcorder ULTIMATE PRO PKG! BRAND NEW!**
   A PACKAGE FOR THE REAL PROS! CHECK IT OUT! $4,399.99 *Buy It Now*   May-25 08:24

Featured items

Another way of improving your sale chances is to choose to have your item featured in certain parts of eBay. This means that your item will appear in more prominent places within the site: either at the top of search results pages or on the eBay home page itself.

There are additional listing fees to have items featured in this way, and in most cases it is probably only worthwhile for items which are going to fetch reasonably high prices. The current fee to have items featured at the top of search results pages is $19.95 (Featured Plus!) and to have them on the home page is $39.95. Therefore it is not worth doing this for items which you think will only fetch a few dollars in an auction. However, for higher priced items it can be a good way to attract more potential buyers and therefore increase the chance of an active and successful auction. To list featured items you have to have an overall feedback rating of 10 or over. Once you have reached this level, the featured items option will be available within the listings page. Until then it will not be available, but there will be a link giving you more information:

If you are using eBay to conduct an online business it may be worth assessing whether the additional fee of having a featured item would be cost-effective in terms of overall profit.

Viewing Featured Plus! items

To view items that are featured at the top of search results:

Click on a category item, or enter a keyword into the search box

2 The featured items are displayed at the top of the search results page. By default, they appear with the auctions most recently listed at the top

Non-featured items can still have bold and highlighting added to them for emphasis.

3 Scroll down the page to see the non-featured items. There is normally a line that divides the featured and non-featured items

Viewing home page featured items

Items that are featured on the eBay home page are displayed in a separate box:

1 Click on an item to go directly to that auction

2 Click here to view all of the home page featured items

Home page featured items rotate in the home page box, because there are too many of them to be displayed at once.

3 All of the home page featured items are listed. By default, they appear with the auctions ending soonest at the top

Conducting an auction

Once an auction starts it is important to be in a position to monitor and manage it, to deal with any problems that occur and to try to maximize the amount of money from the sale. This chapter looks at what happens when an auction starts and how to deal with questions from prospective buyers. It also shows you how to amend and improve listings during the course of an auction and explains the post-auction procedure in terms of getting paid and shipping items.

Covers

Chapter Eight

Once an auction starts

When an auction in which you are selling something starts, you can just sit back and wait until the end of the auction to see what happens and what price has been achieved for the item. However, for a more successful eBay career it is important to keep an eye on the auction to see how it is progressing and, if necessary, give it some added impetus. Initially there are two things that you should do once you have completed listing an item and the auction has started:

1 Conduct a search for the item to make sure it has been registered in the eBay database of items for sale. This can take a few hours, since the database is updated throughout the day. The item should have a sunrise icon next to it, indicating that it is a new listing. Click on the link for your item to view the actual auction page

If you have set the duration of the auction for the maximum amount of time (10 days), your item will initially be at the end of the search results list – by default, this is sorted by auctions ending soonest. However, if you have set the duration for a shorter time then your item will appear in between other current auctions.

2 Check on the auction page to make sure the listing and image are as they should be. You can

also check here periodically to see the number of bids that have been made (this will also be visible on your My eBay page)

Answering questions

It is important to be available during an auction so that you can answer any questions that prospective buyers might have. These could be anything from asking about the shipping arrangements, to requesting more information about the technical specification of an item. A good seller will always try to answer questions as quickly and as honestly as possible. If you leave a question unanswered then the prospective buyer will probably not proceed with a bid.

1   When a prospective buyer asks a question, it will be flagged up on the auction page (which only you can see) and you will also be sent an email with the question

Questions for Photoshop Elements 3

See item description
Please respond to the question below from   . eBay will send an email to the buyer for you.

Q: Is the book the US version?

    Type your response here.

Need help calculating shipping cost? Use the Shipping Calculator

Enter up to 1000 characters. HTML cannot be displayed.

☐ Display this question and response on my listing so all buyers can see it. Once posted, it can't be edited.
☐ Hide my email address for privacy purposes.

[Submit response]   Delete

2   Enter your reply here

Questions for Photoshop Elements 3

See item description
Please respond to the question below from   . eBay will send an email to the buyer for you.

Q: Is the book the US version?

    Yes, it is the latest US version, in full color.

Need help calculating shipping cost? Use the Shipping Calculator

Enter up to 1000 characters. HTML cannot be displayed.

☑ Display this question and response on my listing so all buyers can see it. Once posted, it can't be edited.
☑ Hide my email address for privacy purposes.

[Submit response]   Delete

3   Click here to send your reply

If you have several selling auctions on the go at the same time make sure you answer any questions in relation to the correct one.

Promoting items

If an auction for a particular item is not going well – for example, if you have had no bids for it – you can still return to the original listing page and add some promotional functions, to try to boost the item's appeal. To add promotional items to an existing auction:

1   Open the relevant auction page and click here to promote an item

Photoshop Elements 3

You are signed in

Seller status: Your item has been bid up to US $2.30

You have 1 question to answer

NEW! Change your cross-promoted items

Revise your item

Promote your item

Sell a similar item

The options for promoting an existing auction are the same as those for a listing when it is first made.

2   The available options are listed here

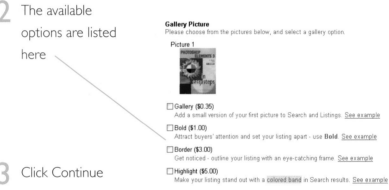

Gallery Picture
Please choose from the pictures below, and select a gallery option.

Picture 1

☐ Gallery ($0.35)
   Add a small version of your first picture to Search and Listings. See example

☐ Bold ($1.00)
   Attract buyers' attention and set your listing apart - use **Bold**. See example

☐ Border ($3.00)
   Get noticed - outline your listing with an eye-catching frame. See example

☐ Highlight ($5.00)
   Make your listing stand out with a colored band in Search results. See example

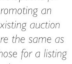

The Gallery option for a picture can be used to place a thumbnail of the image next to the title on the results page when an item is searched for.

3   Click Continue

4   Select any options for promoting your auction and click Continue down the page

Increase your item's visibility

Preview your listing in search results

	Item Title	PayPal	Price	Bids	Time Listed▼
	This is an example with Gallery	🅟	**$x.xx**	-	May-25 07:33
>>	Photoshop Elements 3	🅟	**$2.30**	3	May-25 07:36
	This is an example with Bold		**$x.xx**	-	May-25 07:39

Revising listings

As well as adding new promotional details to an existing auction, it is also possible to edit some of the details, such as the title, the description, and the shipping charges, or to list the item under a second category. Revisions can be made if there have been no bids for an item and there is more than 12 hours left until the end of the auction. If your item has received a bid, or there is less than 12 hours left, then you can only add to the description or add promotional items. To revise a listing:

Adding a listing to an additional category means that there is more chance of users finding it during a search. However, you will have to pay two insertion fees, one for each category.

1 Open the relevant auction page and click here to revise it

2 The available options are shown here

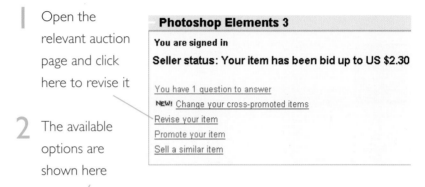

Photoshop Elements 3

You are signed in

Seller status: Your item has been bid up to US $2.30

You have 1 question to answer
NEW! Change your cross-promoted items
Revise your item
Promote your item
Sell a similar item

Once an item has been revised, this is noted on the auction page, to alert potential buyers to this fact.

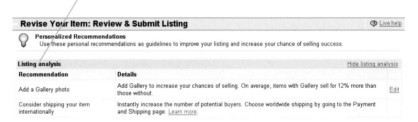

Revise Your Item: Review & Submit Listing   Live help

Personalized Recommendations
Use these personal recommendations as guidelines to improve your listing and increase your chance of selling success.

Listing analysis   Hide listing analysis

Recommendation	Details	
Add a Gallery photo	Add Gallery to increase your chances of selling. On average, items with Gallery sell for 12% more than those without.	Edit
Consider shipping your item internationally	Instantly increase the number of potential buyers. Choose worldwide shipping by going to the Payment and Shipping page. Learn more.	

3 Click Continue further down the page

4 Scroll through the listing until you find the element to change

Second Category   Add second Category

Title & Description   Add to description

5 Edit the selected element of a listing

Add to description ∗

> Ideal for beginners and also users who have a
> general understanding of image editing.

Enter <p> to start a new paragraph. Get more HTML tips.

Spell check | Preview description

Note: Since your original listing either has bids or ends within 12 hours, you

Note: After you click **Continue**, you may be asked to download a small file.
next page does not appear, change your picture selection method.

If a prospective buyer has asked a question about a listing, such as the amount for shipping, this could be used as the basis for reviewing and revising the listing. However, make sure the request is reasonable.

Cancel Changes | Save Changes

If you agree to change a listing in response to a request from a user, make sure you change the actual listing rather than agree the change directly with the other person.

6 Click Save Changes

7 Click Submit Revisions to update the existing listing

Cancel Revision | Submit Revisions

When an auction finishes

When an auction of your own is in progress it can be a nerve-wracking process just waiting to see if you get any bids at all for your item. As long as you get at least one bid (and you have not put a reserve price on the item) you will be able to sell the item to the highest bidder at the end of the auction. Once this happens you will have to perform a few tasks to help the buyer pay you so that they can receive the item:

If an item has no bids, and therefore no buyers, you will have the chance to relist it for sale. This will involve paying the listing fees again. If you do relist an item, take a critical look at the original listing to see if there are any ways in which it could be improved.

1 Once the auction finishes, you will be sent an email notifying you of the winning bidder. Click here to send them payment details

If the person who has won an auction does not pay you or backs out of the transaction, you can offer it to the second-highest bidder. This is known as a Second Chance Offer.

2 Alternatively, go to the auction page and click here

As well as an invoice sent by the seller, a buyer will also be sent payment details automatically by eBay.

3 Enter any payment or returns details here

Enter Payment Instructions & Personal Message

Give clear instructions to assist buyers with payment.

> Return within 30 days if goods damaged or faulty on arrival.

Note: 500 character limit

☑ Copy me on this email

(Send)

After you click this button, your buyer will be emailed an invoice.

4 Click Send to send the invoice to the buyer

5 The invoice is sent to the buyer, who can use it to make the payment by clicking on the Pay Now button

Receiving payment

From the seller's point-of-view, the most important part of a transaction is getting paid. In some cases the buyer will just send the payment once they have been notified that they have won the auction. If this happens, it is just a matter of waiting until you receive the payment before sending off the item. In other instances, the buyer may contact you to ask exactly how you would like payment:

1   If a buyer sends an email enquiring about payment, you will be able to give them exact details by replying to the message

From:
Subject: **ref: eBay purchase - item**
Date: 12:41:54 AM GMT+01:00
To: Nick Vandome

Hello

How would you like me to pay?

Regards

If you have a PayPal account and you receive a credit card payment to it, you will need to upgrade to the Premier PayPal account in order to accept and access this payment. This is looked at in more detail in Chapter Ten.

2   If you are receiving payment via PayPal, you will be sent an email confirmation once the funds have been paid

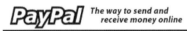 **The way to send and receive money online**

Dear Nick Vandome,

This email confirms that you have received a $13.05 USD from

View the details of this transaction here:

Shipping items

The two golden rules about shipping items are:

Although books, CDs and DVDs can be sent in ordinary envelopes, it shows the buyer that you have made the extra effort if you send them in a padded envelope.

- Take the items to a post office and get them weighed before you list them for sale. This way you will not get a nasty shock at the time of shipping. If you have to pay more for shipping than you charged the buyer then it is a waste of money. Conversely, do not overcharge for shipping: find out the correct amount and then charge this, or slightly more to take into account the cost of packaging and your own time.

- Package items in a way in which you would like to receive something yourself. If the buyer sees that you have made an effort with the packaging then they will be more likely to leave you positive feedback and also to buy from you again.

Depending on the type of item you are shipping, there are different alternatives for packaging. If in doubt, use more packaging rather than less.

- Brown paper and string. If you are sending non-breakable items, such as clothes, then one option would be to package them as a parcel with brown paper and string. If you do this, make sure there are at least a couple of layers of paper, in case one layer gets torn.

- Padded envelopes. There are a variety of padded envelopes available at most post offices. These are ideal for items such as books, CDs and DVDs.

Courier services are also a good option for delivery of items. Some to look at are:
DHL at www.dhl.com
CitiPak at www.citipak.com
FedEx at www.federalexpress.com

- Boxes. Different sized boxes can be bought at the post office, but it is also a good idea to collect boxes, such as shoeboxes, for use when sending eBay items to buyers.

- Bubble wrap. This can be bought in a large roll and it is ideal for wrapping items and also for using to pack boxes.

- Additional packaging. Other useful items for packing boxes include newspaper and the polystyrene that comes in packaging for items such as televisions and computers.

Feedback

Feedback from eBay users following transactions is vital to the smooth running of the site. This is used to assess how trustworthy, or otherwise, users are and it is an invaluable tool in the self-regulation process. This chapter explains the types of feedback on eBay, shows how to view and leave feedback and also covers the essential issue of giving and receiving negative feedback.

Covers

Chapter Nine

Why feedback matters

Unlike a lot of websites where there is a rarely used option for leaving feedback or comments, the feedback mechanism on eBay is vital to the continuing success of the site. Feedback is actively encouraged from both buyers and sellers for all transactions. The amount of feedback appears next to a User's ID and all other registered eBay users can access this feedback to see what has been said about someone.

We all like to hear what other people think about us but on eBay feedback is a lot more than idle curiosity: it informs buyers and sellers about people's track records on eBay and how they perform when they are conducting transactions. In effect, it is an extremely effective method of self-regulation by eBay users. If a buyer or a seller is acting in an unprofessional or dishonest way then this will quickly show up in the feedback, and their eBay career may come to a swift end. Some points to remember about feedback:

It is possible to block your feedback from other users, but this is not recommended as it suggests you have something to hide. You can block your feedback by visiting the Help section. Then type Feedback Private into the search engine and you will be taken to a page where you can hide your feedback. However, this only applies to the feedback comments, not your overall feedback profile. Always think carefully before dealing with anyone who has elected to have their feedback hidden.

- There are three types of feedback that can be given: positive, neutral and negative.

- Feedback stays with you throughout your eBay career. There are certain, rare circumstances when feedback can be removed, but in general your feedback sticks to you like glue.

- Feedback is usually available for all other users to read and evaluate. Your feedback is visible to everyone else and you can check the feedback of everyone else too.

- You can give feedback only after you have completed a transaction (bought or sold something).

- Feedback should be honest, accurate and informative. Essentially, feedback is for the benefit of other eBay users, so they can decide if they want to deal with this user. Try to make your feedback worthwhile and informative.

- When making a transaction with another eBay user always, always read the feedback that has been left about them. If there is anything untoward, it will show up there.

Types of feedback

Positive feedback

This is the most common type of feedback and is given by both a buyer and a seller if a transaction goes smoothly: when the buyer pays promptly, the seller sends the goods promptly and they are just as they are described in the auction. This type of feedback makes up the vast majority that is left on eBay. Technically, a seller should be in a position to leave feedback before a buyer, as they will receive payment before the goods are despatched. In reality, some sellers wait until they have received feedback from the buyer before leaving some of their own.

Positive feedback can be left by both a buyer and a seller

A good way to quickly build up positive feedback is to buy cheap items that can be delivered online. An ideal area for this is recipes. If the seller accepts PayPal, then the whole operation can be completed within a few minutes, including the receiving and leaving of feedback.

 Excellent buyer, very quick payment, very highly recommended

Neutral feedback

This is the least common type of feedback and is left when either a buyer or a seller is not entirely happy with a transaction. It might be because one element of the deal was unsatisfactory, such as a description of an item being slightly inaccurate, while the rest of it was conducted as expected. This is a bit of a gray area on eBay and, in reality, most users have fairly strong opinions when it comes to feedback: they either like the way a transaction has been handled or they don't. However, neutral feedback comments should be read carefully to see what the issue was and whether you feel this would effect your dealings with the person involved.

Negative feedback

This is the most serious type of feedback as it indicates a problem with a transaction. This could be for a variety of reasons; from payment not being sent, to fraud where a seller accepts payment for an item and then does not send it. In cases like this, the amount of negative feedback generated would ensure the person involved would not prosper on eBay for long. However, until the feedback appears they may still get away with it for a few transactions. Negative feedback is a serious issue on eBay and you should always think twice before you leave any, and strive to ensure that you have none left for yourself.

For more on negative feedback, see pages 153–155.

Accessing feedback

It is possible to access feedback for all registered eBay users and also to view the feedback that has been left about you by other people. To view other users' feedback click on their User ID wherever it appears, such as on an auction page. You can view your own feedback through your My eBay page or via your User ID.

Viewing feedback on the My eBay page

1 Open your My eBay page and click here to access your own feedback

My Account
- Personal Information
- Addresses
- Manage Subscriptions
- eBay Preferences
- Feedback
- Seller Account
- PayPal Account

It is not obligatory to leave feedback, so don't be offended if someone does not leave you any even after you have left some for them.

2 This icon denotes that feedback has been left for a particular item

3 The most recent feedback is displayed on your My eBay page

Items Awaiting Feedback (3 items)					
Title	User ID	Sale Date ▽	Action		
3600 RECIPES E-Book Free ship! DELIVERED IN MINUTES! (4382942094)		May-25-05 05:37:28	Leave Feedback	☆	⊕
BRAND NEW APPLE IPOD SHUFFLE 512MB MP3 PLAYER (5775826599)		May-25-05 05:20:50	Leave Feedback	☆	⊕
Brand New Hoya 67mm UV guard glass filter for D70 (7517255253)		May-25-05 03:58:28	Leave Feedback	☆	○

Legend: ☆ Feedback Left ○ Feedback Received

Back to top

Page 1 of 1

Recent Feedback (View all feedback)			
Comment	From	Date/Time	Item #
⊕ FAST PAYMENT !!! GOOD BUYER !!!	Seller:	May-27-05 09:41	5775826599
⊕ Great buyer...prompt payment, valued customer, highly recommended.	Seller:	May-25-05 03:17	4382942094

Viewing feedback via User ID

To view all of your feedback via your User ID:

Viewing your own feedback via the User ID is just the same as viewing the feedback for another user.

1 Click here on your own User ID

Hello, <u>nickvan1</u> (16 ☆) me

2 The current feedback score is shown here

The feedback score is the aggregate of positive and negative feedback. The positive feedback figure is a percentage of positive feedback in relation to all of the feedback you have received.

Member Profile: nickvan1 (16 ☆) me

| Feedback Score: | 16 |
| Positive Feedback: | 100% |

Members who left a positive:	16
Members who left a negative:	0
All positive feedback received:	16

<u>Learn about</u> what these numbers mean.

Recent Ratings:

	Past Month	Past 6 Months	Past 12 Months
⊕ positive	2	2	16
◉ neutral	0	0	0
⊖ negative	0	0	0

Bid Retractions (Past 6 months) 0

3 A summary of feedback for the last 12 months is shown here

4 Scroll down the page to see all of the feedback comments

Click on the tabs along the top of the feedback window to view feedback from just buyers, just sellers or feedback you have left for others.

| **Feedback Received** | From Buyers | From Sellers | Left for Others |

16 feedback received by nickvan1 (0 mutually withdrawn)

Comment

⊕ FAST PAYMENT !!! GOOD BUYER !!!

⊕ Great buyer...prompt payment, valued customer, highly recommended.

⊕ Item delivered speedily and in good condition. Good contact too.

⊕ good value, good fast delevery, hope to do business again.thanks

⊕ great buyer, fast payment, good transaction - thanks

⊕ Prompt PayPal payment. Clear comms. Can't get better. ▭ recommends A+++

⊕ Great communication. A pleasure to do business with.

⊕ Quick payment. Excellent ebayer. Perfect! THANKS!!

Giving feedback

Whenever you are involved in a transaction it is good manners to leave feedback for the other person. This is not only polite, it also helps the rest of the eBay community assess the performance of the other person. To leave feedback:

Feedback reminders are automatically placed on your My eBay page once you have completed a transaction.

1 Go to your My eBay page and click here

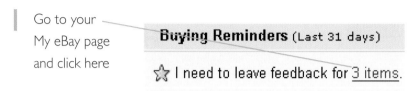

Buying Reminders (Last 31 days)

⭐ I need to leave feedback for 3 items.

2 Alternatively, go to the Items I've Won section on your My eBay page and click here

You can also leave feedback by going to the original auction page once it has finished and following the feedback link there.

Shipping Cost	Sale Date	Action	$	⭐	💬
$4.50	May-25	Leave Feedback ▼	$	☆	💬

3 Use these buttons to select the type of feedback to leave

User ID:	
Item Number:	
Rating:	⦿ Positive ○ Neutral ○ Negative ○ I will leave feedback later
Comment:	Excellent communication and very fast delivery. Highly recommended
	14 characters left.

Show all transactions

[Leave Feedback] Cancel

4 Enter your comments (up to 80 characters) and click the Leave Feedback button

Negative feedback

Since most of eBay's business is based on trust between the users, negative feedback is a serious issue. It can result in prospective buyers steering clear of a particular auction and, ultimately, ruining someone's eBay career. Negative feedback is like a very public black mark against your name. In many cases this can be justified – reasons for leaving negative feedback include:

- Buyers not paying any money once they have won an auction.

- Sellers not sending items once they have received payment.

- Goods being delivered but being nothing like their description in the auction.

Never threaten another user with negative feedback as a means to gain an advantage in some way. This could get you banned from eBay.

- Rude or obstructive behavior when a buyer has tried to get more information from a seller.

However, there are some cases where negative feedback is not always justified:

- Genuine mistakes. These do occur and negative feedback can be left as a result of an unavoidable mix up, such as an item being lost in the post.

- Mischief makers. Some people will deliberately leave negative feedback to inconvenience people. Since all users are allowed to leave feedback after a transaction has been completed there is not much that can be done about this, except to try to answer the feedback in a rational and even-handed way.

- Retaliatory negative feedback. Sometimes when a user leaves negative feedback the other person will do the same just out of spite (as long as they have not already left feedback). This is frequently unjustified but, again, there is not much that can be done about stopping it.

Try to reduce the chances of negative feedback by paying promptly for purchases, sending sold items quickly (in the described condition) and communicating effectively with users.

Leaving negative feedback

Just as you should strive to not have any negative feedback left about yourself, so leaving negative feedback for others should be a last resort. If you are unhappy about a transaction, take time to evaluate the situation before giving negative feedback:

● If an item you have received is not how you think it should be, go back to the auction page and check the description, just to make sure that you have not missed anything.

● Check to see whether the person with whom you are dealing is a new eBay user. Some new users do not understand fully how the site works and this can result in misunderstandings.

● If an item that you have bought and paid for is not delivered, or no payment is sent for an item that you have sold, contact the other user to ask them about it. This can be done by clicking on their User ID to view their user profile and then clicking on the Contact Member button. Make sure you are polite and business-like in your message and that you convey the exact nature of your concern.

If a user does not reply to your email queries, you could try the Square Trade mediation service, which is looked at on page 180.

● Leave a reasonable amount of time once you have contacted the other person. Do not expect an instant reply: a period of three days is an acceptable amount of time to wait.

If you have explored these avenues and you are still dissatisfied then you may have no choice but to leave negative feedback. Some people do not like doing this, as they feel it could result in retaliatory feedback from the other person; but, if you have a justified case, it is important that you do leave negative feedback. It is not a case of seeking revenge, it is about helping other eBay users come to a decision about whether to deal with this person or not. In some cases, you may be helping people avoid someone who should not be conducting business on eBay.

Negative feedback is left in the same way as leaving positive or neutral feedback. However, you are responsible for your comments, so make sure you are not abusive, defamatory or libellous. Make your point honestly and dispassionately, in a way that voices your concerns and alerts other users.

Replying to negative feedback

If you do receive negative feedback, for whatever reason, you are entitled to reply to it and it is important that you do so. Otherwise the negative comments will remain there unanswered and other users will think that you agree with the criticism and accept it. Once negative feedback is received, you will be alerted and given the chance to respond. However, before you do so, there are some points to bear in mind:

You can reply to negative feedback only once, so make sure your response is as effective as possible, and try to avoid being too confrontational.

- Have a look at the user profile of the person giving the negative feedback. This will display the feedback that they have received and also the feedback they have left for others. You may discover that they are a serial leaver of negative feedback or that their own feedback rating is very poor. If this is the case you can mention it when you reply to the negative feedback that they have left you.

- Check the negative feedback to see if there is any truth in it. If there is, then be honest about this when you reply.

- If the negative feedback is retaliatory – in reply to negative feedback that you have posted about the other user – note this in your reply, as tactfully as possible.

Never use abusive language when replying to negative feedback, regardless of what the other person has said about you.

- Leave it a day or two before you reply to negative feedback. The immediate reaction to being criticized is to fire off a strongly worded retort. However, it is better to look at it calmly so you are not replying out of anger.

- Since you only have one opportunity to reply, you should choose your words carefully so that they address the criticism rather than insult the other user.

The receipt of negative feedback can be unpleasant but it does not have to be disastrous. If you play fair and approach any criticism in the appropriate manner then some negative feedback should not have a detrimental effect on your eBay career. Most eBayers are proficient at tracking down suspicious users, and if you reply fairly and accurately to any negative feedback then you should not have too much to worry about in the long term.

Withdrawing feedback

In exceptional circumstances eBay will let you withdraw feedback, but only with the consent of the other user. You might withdraw feedback because of a genuine misunderstanding or if you left the feedback for the wrong person by mistake (however, if this happens, you have to leave the feedback for the correct person as soon as it has been withdrawn). To withdraw feedback:

1 Contact the other person involved and agree that you want to mutually withdraw an item of feedback

2 Go to the Help section and enter Feedback Withdrawal into the search engine. From the results, select the relevant page and click the Online Form link

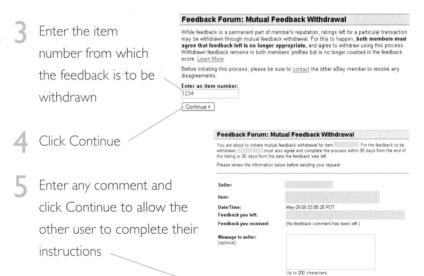

The Mutual Feedback Withdrawal Process
After both parties have agreed to withdraw the feedback, both parties will have their feedback scores adjusted at the same time. Depending on the type of feedback withdrawn, each party's score could increase, decrease or remain the same. eBay will add a note to the feedback comment, saying that the feedback was mutually withdrawn.

Note: If you haven't left feedback for your trading partner and you go through the Mutual Feedback Withdrawal process, you will no longer be able to leave feedback for that transaction.

You may only request Mutual Feedback Withdrawal once for every feedback left. You should only make such requests if both you and the other person have already agreed to have the feedback removed in advance.

Important: Members may initiate a request to mutually withdraw feedback within 30 days of either person leaving feedback or within 90 days of the transaction end date, whichever is later.

Want to start the Mutual Feedback Withdrawal process? Go to our online form.

If you have not found the information you are looking for, please ask a question.

Every auction has an item number, which can be found on the auction page, next to the item title.

3 Enter the item number from which the feedback is to be withdrawn

Feedback Forum: Mutual Feedback Withdrawal

While feedback is a permanent part of member's reputation, ratings left for a particular transaction may be withdrawn through mutual feedback withdrawal. For this to happen, **both members must agree that feedback left is no longer appropriate,** and agree to withdraw using this process. Withdrawn feedback remains in both members' profiles but is no longer counted in the feedback score. Learn More

Before initiating this process, please be sure to contact the other eBay member to resolve any disagreements.

Enter an item number:
1234

[Continue >]

4 Click Continue

5 Enter any comment and click Continue to allow the other user to complete their instructions

Feedback Forum: Mutual Feedback Withdrawal

You are about to initiate mutual feedback withdrawal for item [   ]. For the feedback to be withdrawn, [   ] must also agree and complete the process within 90 days from the end of the listing or 30 days from the date the feedback was left.

Please review the information below before sending your request.

Seller:
Item:
Date/Time: May-25-05 03:58:26 PDT
Feedback you left:
Feedback you received: (No feedback comment has been left.)
Message to seller: (optional)

Up to 200 characters.

[Continue >] Cancel request

Financial matters

Sooner or later all eBay users will have to confront the financial side of operating on the site, whether it is as a buyer or a seller. This chapter looks at some of these matters, including the amount of eBay fees and who has to pay them, the methods of payment and a comprehensive look at the online payment service PayPal. It also looks at the type of protection that is offered to buyers, and escrow services that can be used for holding payments until a transaction has completed.

Covers

eBay fees

eBay makes its money by charging users to list items for sale and also by taking a percentage fee of the final sale price. The insertion fee is based on the starting price for an item, and the seller is responsible for paying both the listing fee and the final value fee. The current insertion fees are:

The insertion fee is the fee for placing an item for sale on eBay. The listing fee is the overall fee that includes additional items such as featured items and extra pictures.

- $0.01 to $0.99, insertion fee is $0.25

- $1.00 to $9.99, insertion fee is $0.35

- $10.00 to $24.99, insertion fee is $0.60

- $25.00 to $49.99, insertion fee is $1.20

- $50.00 to $199.99, insertion fee is $2.40

- $200.00 to $499.99, insertion fee is $3.60

- $500.00 or more insertion fee is $4.80

If you are selling real estate on eBay, the insertion fees range between $35.00 to $300.00 depending on the type of property and the type of advertisement used.

The current final value fees are:

- Item not sold, no fee.

- $0.01 to $25.00, the final value fee is 5.25% of the amount of the high bid.

Prices given in this book were correct at time of going to press.

- $25.01 to $1000.00, the final value fee is 5.25% of the first $25.00 ($1.31), plus 2.75% of the remaining balance.

- Over $1000.01, the final value fee is 5.25% of the first $25.00 ($1.31), plus 2.75% of the next $25.01 to $1000.00 ($26.81) plus 1.50% of the remaining balance.

If an item is given a reserve price the fee is $1.00 if the reserve price is $1.00 to $49.99; $2.00 if the reserve price is $50.00 to $199.99; and 1% of the reserve price if it is $200.00 or more. The maximim fee for a reserve price item is $100.00.

Methods of payment

There are several ways in which goods can be paid for on eBay. If you are selling items, you will have the option of selecting the payment methods which you are prepared to accept. If you are a buyer you will be able to see the accepted payment methods on the auction page. The methods of payment on eBay are:

 Any type of payment is subject to the possibility of fraud. If you are uncertain about any type of payment, contact the seller for clarification. If you are still in doubt, do not proceed with the transaction.

- Electronic payment. This is where an online payment is made through a third party. On eBay the most common form of electronic payment is through PayPal, which is looked at in more detail on the following pages.

- Check. A personal check can be used to pay for items. However, this takes longer as the seller should wait until the check has been cleared before sending the goods.

 Never make payments through an instant cash wire transfer service such as Western Union or MoneyGram, particularly if this is the only method of payment offered. It means that you effectively pay cash, without any guarantee that the goods will be delivered.

- Credit card. Some sellers accept direct payments by credit card. However, if you are a seller this can involve charges for each credit card transaction.

- Postal order or money order. This is a way of sending money without using cash or a check. They can be purchased at post offices or banks but there is usually a charge to cash them.

- Escrow. This is a service where a company holds payment for an item until the transaction has been completed. It is looked at in more detail on page 166.

 Cash On Delivery (COD) can be an option for payment, but only if the goods are being delivered in person by the seller. This could be if they live near to the buyer and it should only really be used after contact between the two parties.

- Bank transfer. This is where money is transferred directly from one bank account to another. There is usually some form of charge attached.

For all of these methods of payments, eBay offers some level of protection against fraudulent transactions. Under the standard purchase protection programme, payments are covered up to $200 (minus $25 processing costs).

It is strongly recommended that cash is never used as a method of payment: it can easily be stolen in transit and it is untraceable if the seller does not send the purchased item.

About PayPal

PayPal is an online electronic payment service and it is eBay's preferred method of payment for buyers and sellers. The company was bought by eBay in 2002 and conducts billions of dollars worth of transactions every year. PayPal works by sending funds directly from your PayPal account to the seller of an item. Once you have set up an account (see next page) you can use this to send payments using either your credit card or your bank account, and you can also use it to accept payments from other eBayers if you are selling items.

Once you have set up a PayPal account you can select this as a method of payment when you are listing items for sale. When the auction page is published, this is denoted by the following icon:

After a sale, the money is held in your PayPal account and you can then have it transferred to your own bank account or receive the money as a check. You can also keep the money in your PayPal account and use this for future purchases on eBay.

Despite some of the issues connected with PayPal, it is still a very effective and efficient way of completing transactions on eBay.

Although PayPal deals with huge amounts of money it is not a bank, and so does not have to comply with the same rules and regulations as traditional financial institutions. This has caused some concerns about customer protection and there have been legal cases to try to ensure greater protection for PayPal customers against fraudulent practices by both buyers and sellers. As a result there have been some improvements to PayPal and the service now offers a Buyer Protection service where qualified purchases are covered up to $1000.00.

If you want to file a claim under the PayPal Buyer Protection service, it has to be made within 30 days of the PayPal payment.

There have also been issues with chargebacks: the system whereby the buyer can claim back money from a purchase if they are not happy with the product. In some cases this has happened when the goods have been perfectly acceptable and the seller has had money removed from their account as a result.

Another PayPal issue concerns the freezing of users' accounts: some people have had their accounts frozen for a considerable period of time after PayPal has suspected them of dubious trading practices.

Registering for PayPal

To use PayPal you have to first register to set up an account. To do this:

1 Go to the PayPal home page at www.paypal.com and click here

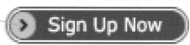

Join PayPal Today
Now over
71 million accounts

> Sign Up Now

Make sure you read the PayPal User Agreement very carefully before you sign up for the service.

2 Select the country in which you live and click Continue

3 Enter your personal details. This will include details of your credit card, which can be used to make payment but at this stage is just used to verify your identity. Select the type of account you require

Sign Up for a PayPal Account

Anyone with an email address can use PayPal to send and receive money online. What is PayPal?

To get started, choose your account type. (All accounts can send payments for FREE.)

○ **Personal Account**
Ideal for online shopping. Send and receive payments for free through PayPal's secure network. Personal accounts cannot accept debit or credit card payments. Learn More

◉ **Premier Account**
Perfect for buying and selling on eBay, e-commerce websites, or via email. Accept all payment types for low fees. Do business under your own name. Learn More

○ **Business Account**
The right choice for your online business. Accept all payment types for low fees. Do business under a company or group name. Learn More

Select the country in which you live:

United States ▾

4 Click here to activate your account

PayPal *The way to send and receive money online*

Activate Your Account.

Dear Nick Vandome,

Congratulations. **You've just created a PayPal account.**

But you've not finished yet.

You must **click the link below** and enter your password on the following page to confirm your email address.

Click here to activate your account

Paying with PayPal

Once you have set up and activated a PayPal account you can use it to pay for items that you have purchased on eBay, as long as the seller accepts this method of payment. You do not have to deposit any money in your PayPal account, as this will be debited from the credit card or bank account details you entered when registering for the service. To make a payment with PayPal:

1 Once you have won an auction the following message appears. Check that PayPal is accepted and click here

Congratulations! You won the item!

Pay Now

Payment methods accepted:

PayPal (MasterCard **VISA** AMEX)

- Personal cheque
- Postal Order or Banker's Draft

↓ Go to Seller's Payment Instructions

When sending money to someone via PayPal some people have a "Confirmed" address. This involves a verification process to prove that the person really does live at the address they claim to.

2 Details of the required payment are displayed

	Qty.	Price	Subtotal
	1	US $11.25	US $11.25

Shipping and handling via USPS Airmail Letter Post: US $4.50
Shipping insurance: (Optional US $ 1.30) Add
Seller discounts (-) or charges (+): Add
Seller Total: US $ 15.75
(recalculate)

☐ I will enter an eBay gift certificate or coupon on PayPal.

Questions about the total? Request total from seller

3 Select PayPal as the method of payment

4 Click Continue

Select a payment method (seller accepts the following)

◉ **PayPal***

MasterCard **VISA** AMEX DISCOVER eCHECK

Up to $1000 of free purchase protection. See eligibility.

◯ Money order / Cashiers check

Continue >

5 Review the payment details

6 Click here if you have not already set up a PayPal account

Payment Details   Secure Transaction 🔒

Item #	Item Title	Qty	Price	Subtotal
5775826599	BRAND NEW APPLE IPOD SHUFFLE 512MB MP3 PLAYER	1	$81.00 USD	$81.00 USD

	US Shipping & Handling via Standard Delivery (includes any seller packing fees) :	$12.00 USD
	US Insurance (not offered):	--
	Total:	**$93.00 USD**

[Edit Payment Details]

If you do not currently have a PayPal account [Click Here]

PayPal Log in

Email Address: nickvandome@mac.co   Forget your email?

PayPal Password: ********   Forget your password?

7 Enter your PayPal login details (which you specified when the account was first created) and click Continue down the page to be taken through the full payment process on the PayPal site

8 Once the payment has been made, you will receive a confirmation email with details of the transaction

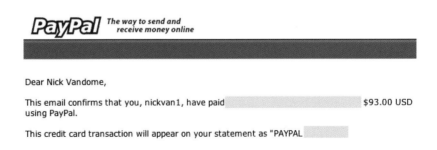

PayPal The way to send and receive money online

Dear Nick Vandome,

This email confirms that you, nickvan1, have paid ▮▮▮▮▮▮▮▮▮ $93.00 USD using PayPal.

This credit card transaction will appear on your statement as "PAYPAL ▮▮▮▮▮

Receiving PayPal payments

If you are selling an item and you have a PayPal account, you can use this to receive payment. However, in some cases you may need to upgrade your account to do so, such as if a user uses a credit card to make a payment to you via PayPal. If this happens, the payment will be marked as Pending in your PayPal account, and also on eBay, and you will have to accept or refuse it. If you accept, you will have to upgrade to a Premier account in order to obtain the payment. If you refuse, the buyer will have to send another form of payment. To accept a payment and upgrade a PayPal account:

For a standard PayPal account it is free to open the account and send and receive funds. It is also free to withdraw funds to US banks.

1 If a payment has been made by credit card, you will be notified and asked if you want to accept or refuse the payment. Select one of the options and click Submit

For a Premier account there are fees for receiving funds. These range from 1.9% plus $0.30 up to 2.9% plus $0.30 depending on the amount received.

2 If you have a standard account you will be taken to a window for upgrading your account, which has to be done in order to obtain the credit card payment. Click here to upgrade

If you already have a Premier Account you still have to accept or reject credit card payments when they are made.

Buyer protection

All buyers on eBay like to know that they are operating in as secure an environment as possible. However, some fraudulent activity does take place and eBay tries to boost user confidence with its Standard Purchase Protection policy. This is offered for all eligible auctions.

Standard Purchase Protection provides the buyer with insurance against being subject to a fraudulent transaction, for example sending money but not receiving the goods. The maximum amount of compensation that they can receive is $200, minus a $25 administration fee. So, if the amount of the item was $200, the buyer would receive only $175. If the amount of the item was $50 the buyer would receive $25: the amount of the claim minus the $25. There are certain criteria that have to be met for this:

If you want additional protection when selling expensive items then an escrow service should be considered, as the Standard Purchase Protection would not offer a high enough level of financial protection. See the next page for details.

- The item was listed and purchased on eBay.

- Both the buyer and seller have positive feedback ratings.

- The item complies with eBay's User Agreement and policies.

- The claim is filed within 90 days of the auction closing.

- You paid for an item and did not receive it, or it was significantly different from the described item.

- No more than 3 claims per 6 months for each user.

- The item was not paid for by cash or an instant cash transfer.

- The item was not lost or damaged in transit.

- The service is not available just because the buyer does not like an item or changes his or her mind.

If you are eligible to claim under the eBay Standard Purchase Protection, you will need to fill in a Standard Purchase Protection claim form and submit proof of payment in order to be reimbursed.

Escrow

Escrow is a type of service that tries to minimize the chance of fraud during an eBay transaction. It works by holding the money until the sale has been completed to the satisfaction of both parties. In general there are five steps in a transaction that makes use of escrow:

1   The buyer and seller agree to use escrow and agree conditions such as the item for sale, its price, the time the buyer has to inspect the item, and the shipping details.

Escrow is a generic term rather than one specific service, even though the eBay-recommended escrow service goes by that name.

2   The buyer pays the escrow service.

3   The seller sends the item.

4   The buyer inspects the item and either accepts or rejects it.

5   The escrow service pays the seller (if the buyer accepted the item).

There are a number of online companies that provide escrow services and the one recommended by eBay is:

Escrow is generally used for expensive items, where there is a considerable risk for both the buyer and the seller.

Escrow.com at www.escrow.com

Most escrow services charge fees based on the value of the item being sold. On Escrow.com there is a fee calculator for working this out. To use this:

There are some fraudulent escrow services that try to entice people into lodging money with them. If you want to use an escrow service then stick to Escrow.com.

1   Enter the currency and amount of the transaction

Escrow Fees And Calculator

For Motor Vehicle Escrow Fees and Services in US.
Click here for more information.

For General Merchandise and Domain Names.

Enter the Transaction Value: $ 200.00   (USD)

[Calculate Your Fee]

Standard Service **Escrow Fee:** $ 25.00   (USD)
Premier Service **Escrow Fee:** $ 25.00   (USD)

2   Click the Calculate Your Fee button to see the final escrow fee for the completed transaction

Operating an eBay business

Thousands of people now make a living solely from buying and selling on eBay. Since there are fewer overheads than for running a "bricks and mortar" retail business, eBay makes it easy for anyone who wants to go into this type of business. This chapter looks at how to prepare an eBay business and shows you how to open your own individual shop on the site. It also deals with managing your auctions and dealing with business issues such as storage, office space and customer service.

Covers

Chapter Eleven

Preparing for business

While many people simply use eBay as a means to clear out their attics and garages, thousands more have created online businesses exclusively on the site. It is possible to make a living from trading on eBay, but if you are thinking of this then you have to approach the whole venture in a professional manner. There are certain areas that you should look at before you start your business:

Business plan

An online eBay business is the same as any other as far as having a business plan is concerned. This is not only essential for any institution from which you want to borrow money, it is also invaluable for getting clear in your own mind what you want to do. Some areas to consider when you are creating a business plan are:

Just because you sell a handful of items on eBay, this does not necessarily mean you will be able to run a successful business. Examine all of the angles very carefully and consider all of the things that could go wrong.

- The type of product or products you are going to sell and how you are going to source them.

- The money required for the initial investment, which could include the products to sell, office space and warehouse space.

- The amount of time you are able to commit to the eBay business (a lot of eBay businesses are run by people who are also working in another job).

In theory, all income generated on eBay is subject to income tax. This is particularly relevant if you are operating as a business. However, if you are only selling a few items as a hobby and for a small amount of money, you may not have to worry about tax. If in doubt, check with an accountant.

- Estimated income and expenditure, in both the short-term and long-term. Make sure that these estimates are realistic, both for your own sake and also for any potential investors.

Several business enterprise organizations or local authorities offer advice about setting up a small business, including details about creating a business plan.

Initial investment

The main reason for creating a business plan is to borrow money from a financial institution. Their chief concern will be whether they will be able to get back any investment which they make. As a potential eBay business person, your first task is to decide how much money you will need to set up and run your business. In some cases you may be able to finance this yourself (at least initially) or to persuade family or friends to invest in your business.

Always be careful when borrowing money from family and friends: what might seem like a great idea in the excitement of a new venture can turn sour once the realities of the business world start to bite.

If you do go to a bank or a financial institution for a loan, arrange a personal meeting so that you can discuss your idea and business plan face-to-face with someone. Do not over-extend yourself in terms of the amount of money you borrow, and make sure you ask questions of the financial institution, such as how much they will charge for the loan and the fees that will be charged on a business bank account (if you set up one). In some cases, the lender may ask for some form of collateral, but try and avoid this by limiting the amount you want to borrow.

Being professional on eBay

If you are looking to operate an eBay business then you have to do this in as professional a manner as possible: if you are looking to make it more than a hobby then you have to treat it as such. This includes:

- Making your listings as professional as possible in terms of product descriptions and accompanying photographs. Consider the descriptions as an exercise in copywriting and look at some other eBay businesses to see how they approach this. Another way of making your listings more business-like is to create your own eBay store, and this is looked at on the following pages.

Although it costs money to employ lawyers and accountants this could save you money in the long term. A lawyer could help resolve financial disputes and an accountant could make you aware of expenses for which you can claim. Also, fees for professional services such as these are tax-deductible as business expenses.

- Decide how you want to set up your business in terms of having a sole ownership, a partnership or a limited liability company. This will depend on the size of the prospective business and the number of people who are going to be involved with it.

- Find a lawyer who is a specialist in business law. This will not only help you if there are any disputes once you start your business, but they will also be able to give you advice about setting up the business.

- Find an accountant. If you are serious about trading commercially on eBay then it is important to have someone to do the financial books and deal with thorny issues such as tax. You can do this yourself, but it saves a lot of time and effort to employ a professional.

Inventory

The inventory for an eBay business is basically the items that are going to be sold. These can be sourced from the same areas as for those for individual sales. However, if you are setting up as a business you will probably want a larger volume of items than for an individual seller. Some areas for obtaining inventory include:

If you are planning to sell a large number of similar items as part of a business, do some test auctions first, to see if there is a market for these items and, if so, how much they sell for.

- Manufacturing items yourself. If you have a talent for producing something then you may be able to create a niche market for it on eBay. However, bear in mind that this will eat into your time for running and managing the online side of your eBay business. A good compromise is to find local people who produce exclusive products and then discuss the possibility of setting up a joint business venture.

- Wholesalers. As mentioned on page 94, buying goods in bulk from wholesalers is a good way to obtain a large amount of inventory at reasonable prices.

- Trade shows. Almost every trade is represented, at some point, at a trade show. These are large meeting places for specific trades and they allow companies to show off their products and to sell them to prospective buyers. It is a great way to meet people, to see what is on offer and to make contacts. Be positive and confident, and know what you want to get from people.

Some companies use inventory software to post items on eBay shortly before they reach the end of their shelf lives. This can be a good way of moving unwanted stock before it is too late. One such program (from the German company DeNISys) can be incorporated into the popular business-management software SAP Business One.

- Trade associations. Most trades have equivalent professional associations. If you are interested in a particular trade it could be worth joining its association for contacts and ideas.

- Closeouts, clearances and stocklots. There is a whole industry of companies who buy surplus stock at cheap prices from a variety of retailers. There are a number of reasons for this, such as liquidations, stock that has not sold before a new season starts, or unclaimed freight. A list of some of these companies can be found by typing "closeouts" into Google. It is also possible to do this type of business yourself with local retailers.

Opening an eBay store

Once you have decided on the type of business you want to run and what you will be selling, it is time to think how to present your stock to potential customers. One way to do it is to run numerous individual auctions, but this can be hard to keep track of. A more professional approach is to open your own eBay store. This will then give you a single, business-oriented location for your business. To set up an eBay store:

1 Login and click here on the home page

2 Click here to open a new store

Macromedia, the web authoring software company (now acquired by Adobe), have released a version of their popular program Contribute 3 specifically aimed at eBay users. It enables sellers to author professional shop fronts, without having to know a lot of technical HTML. It is called Contribute 3 for eBay and more information can be found on the Macromedia website at www.macromedia.com/software/contribute/special/ct3_ebay/ (address correct at the time of going to press).

3 Select a design for your store home page

4 Click Continue

5 Click here to select a logo for your store

If you have your own logo, or photographic image, you can add this to your store front by selecting this option and browsing to the file on your hard drive.

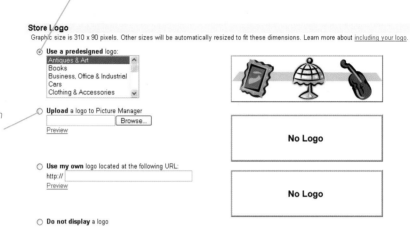

Store Logo

Graphic size is 310 x 90 pixels. Other sizes will be automatically resized to fit these dimensions. Learn more about including your logo.

○ **Use a predesigned** logo:
  - Antiques & Art
  - Books
  - Business, Office & Industrial
  - Cars
  - Clothing & Accessories

○ **Upload** a logo to Picture Manager
  [_____] Browse...
  Preview

○ **Use my own** logo located at the following URL:
  http:// [_____]
  Preview

○ **Do not display** a logo

No Logo

No Logo

6 Scroll down the page and click Continue

It costs a minimum of $15.95 per month to have an eBay store, but this is a small price to pay considering the potential advantages. If you want your store to be more actively promoted it costs more.

7 Select the type of store which you want to create

◉ **Basic Store** ($15.95/month)
A Basic Store is an ideal solution for lower-volume sellers who are just starti

○ **Featured Store** ($49.95/month)
A Featured Store offers all of the benefits of a Basic Store plus eBay's full pr sellers who want to aggressively grow their online business.

○ **Anchor Store** ($499.95/month*)
An Anchor Store offers all of the benefits of a Featured Store plus increased looking for maximum exposure on eBay.

* Free 30-day trial is not available for Anchor Store subscriptions.

8 Click Start My Subscription Now to create your store

How did you hear about this product? [Please select an option ▼]

[Start My Subscription Now >]   Back   Cancel

Auction management software

If you have only ever participated in a few individual auctions you may think that it is easy to keep track of your items, bids, questions and payment options. However, if you are running a commercial venture on eBay you may find that you have dozens, or even hundreds, of auctions running simultaneously. This can lead to stress and confusion as you try to keep up with everything that is going on with your auctions. In a worst-case scenario your business could collapse under the sheer volume of transactions. This is where auction management software can help in automating as much of your eBay activities as possible. Some of the areas which auction management software can handle are:

The My eBay page is a very basic form of auction management software, as it enables you to see details about different auctions in one place.

- Stock control. This keeps a track of what you currently have for sale and what has been sold. As you add more stock, this is updated within the auction management software.

- Auction page creation. Creating standardized auction pages from templates is a great timesaving device and it also helps you to achieve consistency across your auctions.

Auction management software can automate only some of your communication with customers. Sometimes you will have to contact them directly, usually by email. Do not forget the human factor just because the software can do so much.

- Auction management. This keeps a track of all of your auctions so that you can see at a glance what is going on.

- Communication. This is a vital part of eBay and auction management software can take care of filtering your eBay questions, generating automated acknowledgments and sending notification to winning bidders.

Turbo Lister is currently free to download (although it is only available for use with Windows). More details can be found at http://pages. ebay.com/turbo_lister/index.html. Another similar eBay program is Selling Manager.

- Payment. This is another area that can be largely automated by the software. As soon as an auction finishes, automated receipts can be sent to the winning bidder. It is also possible to set up online payment facilities. Shipping details can also be documented by the software.

eBay has its own auction management software, called Turbo Lister. There are also many commercial programs available; one of the market leaders is called Andale. It offers a variety of auction management solutions – more information can be found on the website at www.andale.com

Trading for others

As well as selling your own goods on eBay it is also possible to sell items for other people. People who sell items on behalf of others are known as Trading Assistants. If you want to set yourself up as a Trading Assistant you have to meet the following requirements:

- You must have sold at least 4 items in the last 30 days, to show that you are an active trader on eBay.

- You must have an overall feedback score of 50 or higher.

- You must have an overall positive feedback rating of 97% or higher.

- Your eBay account must be in good standing, with no ongoing disputes or investigations.

Trading Assistants usually trade for themselves as well as for others. This means they frequently have a high turnover of sales and are often Power Sellers.

If you meet these requirements you can register for the Trading Assistants Directory. This can be done as follows:

1 Enter Trading Assistants in the Help search engine

Trading Assistants

Trading Assistants are experienced eBay sellers who, for a fee, will help you sell your items on eBay. You can find a Trading Assistant near you by searching the Trading Assistants Directory. Learn more about how the program works.

2 Scroll down the page and click here

3 Click here to create an entry in the Trading Assistants Directory

Choose a Topic

Find an Assistant
- Basic Search
- **How It Works**
- FAQs

For Trading Assistants
- Create/Edit Your Profile
- Getting Started
- FAQs
- Toolkit

When you register for the Trading Assistants Directory you will have to give details of your service, so prospective clients can see what you offer. This information can include:

When entering your details for the Trading Assistants Directory, be as comprehensive as possible. This is your sales pitch for people who are looking for a Trading Assistant, so ensure you make as compelling a case as possible for them to use you.

- How you will obtain the items from the sellers: whether you are prepared to pick things up or if you have a drop-off point where the sellers can take the goods.

- How much you will charge for selling items. This is usually a percentage of the final selling price.

- Whether the eBay fees are paid up front by the seller or included in the Trading Assistant's fee.

- Types of items which you are prepared to sell. Most Trading Assistants have particular areas of expertise.

- How the item is shipped once it is sold.

- How you are going to pay the seller once the item sells.

- Return and relisting policy (if the item does not sell in the first auction).

Operating as a Trading Assistant

Once you have registered in the Trading Assistants Directory you will be able to start selling for other people. This is done by the seller contacting you via the Trading Assistants Directory and then agreeing either to drop off the item or for you to pick it up. In general it is only really worthwhile if the expected selling price for the item is $50 or over. Once you have the item, you list it on eBay and conduct the auction in the usual way.

As a Trading Assistant you will be subject to the same auction conditions and feedback criteria as if you were conducting an auction for yourself. Although being a Trading Assistant can be more work than running your own auctions, it is an excellent way to supplement your eBay income, particularly if it is used in conjunction with your own eBay store.

Storage and office space

If you are serious about running a retail business on eBay then you will have to give some consideration to how you are going to store items for sale and also where you are going to operate your business from.

It is not a good idea to have too much stock being held in storage at any one time. Try to rotate it as much as possible and avoid creating a backlog of items to sell.

Storage

Initially, you may be able to keep the items you hope to sell on eBay in a spare room or a garage (depending on their size). However, if you are constantly looking to expand your inventory, these options may quickly become unrealistic. If your current storage options start to become cramped, then this could effect your overall operation. Items could be lost or misplaced, resulting in unfulfilled orders and dissatisfied customers. If you are looking for additional storage some of the options could be:

Storage space can also be used to package items before they are sent to customers. However, make sure there is extra room for this with items such as a table and packaging materials close at hand.

- A lock-up garage. These can be rented for monthly or annual fees and provide a good-sized storage facility.

- Commercial storage services. There are companies that offer a variety of storage options such as units, or containers within a warehouse, which can be rented short or long term. Check your local directory or search on the Internet for details.

- An additional shed at home. Garden sheds can be a relatively cheap way to expand your storage options, but make sure you have enough room and that they can be secured if you are going to be storing valuable items in them.

Office space

It is possible to operate an eBay business from the kitchen table, but it is a lot more efficient, and satisfying for all concerned, if you have some dedicated office space. This can be hired commercially but a more realistic option could be to use a spare room and convert it into an office. It does not have to be huge, but make sure it has good lighting, sockets for telephone and computer equipment and adequate shelving for books and paperwork. Also, make sure anyone else living in the house is aware that the room is a work office and not a playroom or an extra TV room. Using a dedicated office can make you feel more professional and you adopt a more business-like approach when you work there.

Thinking globally

eBay really is a global marketplace and if you are operating a business then you should be looking further afield than the markets within your own country. It is perfectly possible to sell your goods anywhere in the world, but there are some points to consider before you start branching out beyond your own shores:

Include exact details about where in the world you are prepared to send items if you are operating globally.

- Local restrictions. Global eBay sites can have different rules concerning what can and cannot be traded, depending on the laws of the country in which they are situated. So it is important to not only comply with the regulations within your own country but also those for the country in which the buyer is located. Make sure you read the user agreements for any countries where you will be doing business.

- Export and import issues. Make sure that you comply with the export conditions for your own country and also the import conditions for the country where the goods are being sent. Your items must clear customs when they are entering a country, so you will have to complete the relevant paperwork when sending items. This could involve a description of the item, where it is being sent and its value. If the item does not clear customs it will be returned to you.

There are a lot of online translation services that will translate text for free. One to try is www.freetranslation.com

- Communication. When you are selling abroad you may be dealing with customers whose first language is different from yours. This can lead to confusion when it comes to communicating with each other. If you are in doubt about anything, get it translated by either an online translation service or an actual translator.

- Payment. The best method for international payment is PayPal, but remember to check the exchange rate for the country involved, to see how much you will receive. Also, PayPal charges a fee for converting between currencies.

- Shipping. Use a recognized mailing service or a courier service, and check that they deliver abroad. It is worth getting shipping insurance, but make sure you include this in the overall shipping charge.

Customer service

Some of the most successful retail companies are the ones with the best customer service. If you are operating your own business on eBay try and emulate this and become known for first-class customer service. The reason for good customer service is not just to ensure that first-time customers are happy with their purchases: the real benefit is in getting these customers to keep returning. Good customer service should be at the top of your list of priorities. Some points to consider are:

When it comes to communicating with buyers, keep calm regardless of any negative or provocative comments they may make. If necessary, it can be better to cut your losses in a dignified manner rather than getting into a protracted slanging match, which could eventually translate into negative feedback.

- Make sure you give people what you say you will. The first step in good customer service is to ensure that what you describe and display in an auction is exactly what the buyer receives. There is no point in trying to hide defects or to exaggerate certain features. These embellishments will be obvious once the buyer gets the item, and then you will have an uphill battle to convince them to buy from you again.

- Communicate quickly and effectively. Answer questions from customers as quickly as possible, so that they can see you are professional and efficient. This will help build up their confidence when dealing with you, which is a vital part of customer service.

- Remember the personal touch. Be friendly when you contact people: use their first names in emails and include a compliment slip when you post items.

- Go the extra mile. Try to accommodate requests from buyers or prospective buyers. Even if it is something that may not immediately gain a sale or make extra money, it could pay off in the longer term if the person comes back to buy something else from you.

- Accept unconditional returns. If you state that you accept returns without any questions asked, buyers will be even more confident about dealing with you. You may come across some people who take advantage of this, but the benefits will outweigh this occasional inconvenience. A lot of successful stores have this type of return policy.

Troubleshooting

Things do go wrong with auctions and with interactions between users on eBay, although this accounts for only a very small percentage of transactions. However, with a little information and planning it is possible to minimize the risks. This chapter looks at some of the problems that can occur and how to avoid them or deal with them.

Covers

Chapter Twelve

Dispute resolution

Due to the number of transactions that take place on eBay it is inevitable that disputes will occur between buyers and sellers. This could be because of defective or fake goods, non-payment, or non-delivery of items. If this happens, buyers can try eBay's own buyer protection service, as detailed in Chapter Ten. Another option, which is recommended by eBay, is to use a dispute resolution service. Their preferred option is Square Trade, which can be found at www.squaretrade.com. The service operates as follows:

- The first party files a complaint against the second party.

- The second party is contacted by Square Trade and told the nature of the dispute.

- The two parties are invited to discuss the dispute within a secure page on the Square Trade site. This is known as "direct negotiation" and there is an option for a Square Trade mediator to help resolve the issue.

- Ideally, the case is resolved to the satisfaction of both parties.

To use the Square Trade service:

1 Visit the website at www.squaretrade.com

2 Click here to start a new dispute resolution case

Trouble with a Purchase or Sales?

❯ **File a Case**

- FREE to file
- Takes only 5 minutes!

Help for New Users

3 If a seller displays this symbol, it shows they have met certain Square Trade criteria for fair trading

Before using a dispute resolution service such as Square Trade, try hard to resolve any problems directly with the other party.

Scams and frauds

In any walk of life, large sums of money will attract criminals and con artists. eBay is no different in this respect and some individuals undertake fraudulent activities on the site. However, that said, fraud forms only a tiny percentage of the overall volume of sales, and you are probably as secure trading on eBay as you are in any other retailing environment. The type of frauds that can occur on eBay are:

Legally, fraud on eBay is just the same as in any other walk of life, and people who commit fraud are liable to criminal prosecution.

- Non-delivery of goods. This is the most obvious fraud, and the one that users (particularly new users) are most worried about. This is a relatively simple fraud, whereby the seller takes payment for an item and never sends it. Thankfully, due to the robust feedback system on eBay, these individuals do not last long on the site. However, they can have time to make a number of fraudulent transactions before they are caught out. As a buyer all you can do is try to investigate sellers as fully as possible from their feedback before you make a payment. If you are in any doubt about the type or amount of feedback they have then do not proceed.

If you are subjected to a fraud, report it in the first instance to eBay via the buyer protection service. Also, depending on the amount involved, you may want to consider reporting it to the police.

- Long-term fraud. Some individuals have the patience to spend months building up positive feedback and a good trading background on eBay. Then they start taking payment and not sending the goods. Since the feedback may not offer any clue to the buyer, try looking at the types of items that are for sale. If someone has been selling low priced items and then they suddenly start selling much more expensive ones, this could be a warning sign.

- Selling links rather than products. Some auctions for items look like they are for the actual item, but they turn out to be for a link to a website that may, or may not, offer the item at a bargain price. So essentially you are paying for the possibility of buying the item cheaply. There are a number of these types of auctions (typically for popular electrical items) but personally I would never participate in them. Having said that, a lot of the sellers of these items have high-scoring feedback which suggests they could be genuine, but in general it is better to be safe than sorry.

Spoof emails and websites

Another fraudulent practice directed at eBay is the proliferation of spoof, or fake, emails and websites in recent years. These try to get you to part with your money as part of pyramid selling schemes or pretend to be genuine communications from eBay or PayPal and then ask for your personal login details.

If you have an eBay account and a PayPal account then you will almost certainly receive fake emails sooner or later. Their content will quickly give you an idea of whether they are real or not; if they ask you for money or redirect you to a website that tries to obtain your personal details then they are probably fake. The golden rules about these types of emails are:

The distribution of fake emails and websites is known as "phishing".

- Never part with any money on the promise of making a fortune from pyramid selling.

Fake websites can look convincing in terms of their appearance and the use of eBay and PayPal logos. However, the clues are usually within the content of the pages.

- Never disclose either your eBay or PayPal login details.

- If in doubt about a spoof email, report it to eBay by forwarding it to spoof@ebay.com

Even if emails or websites claim to be genuine and look legitimate, it is almost certain that they are not real if they ask for money or personal details. If in doubt, look at the web address of websites and also view the properties of emails to see if there are any obvious clues there.

Spoof emails should always be ignored, regardless of their content

From:	
Subject:	**Paypal Announcement**
Date:	October 15, 2004 9:09:22 PM GMT+01:00
To:	

and 41 more...

Hello, if you are a paypal user then you really should read this!

How to ▮▮▮▮▮▮▮▮▮ in 30 Days with PayPal!

I WAS SHOCKED WHEN I SAW HOW MUCH MONEY CAME FLOODING INTO MY PAYPAL ACCOUNT??

I turned ▮▮▮▮▮▮ within the first 30 days of operating the business plan that I am about to reveal to you free of charge. If you decide to take action on the following instructions, I will personally GUARANTEE that you will enjoy a similar return!?

Please do not be sceptical about this program. At least think about it for a few days. Otherwise you will be throwing away over ▮▮▮▮ in cash!

Account Guard

One way to increase your security against spoof websites and emails is to use eBay's own Account Guard, which is included in the eBay toolbar. This is a downloadable toolbar that can be used to keep track of your eBay activities. Account Guard is now part of the toolbar, and has a color-coded system to notify you about the status of the website you are visiting:

- Green indicates that you are on a safe eBay or PayPal site.

- Gray indicates that you are probably on a genuine eBay or PayPal site but it might be a fraudulent or spoof site.

- Red indicates that you are probably on a fraudulent site.

At present, the eBay toolbar and Account Guard are only available for Windows. To obtain these:

The eBay toolbar can be used to search for items within eBay, to receive information about ongoing auctions and also to protect your password.

1 Access the eBay Toolbar page from the Help search box

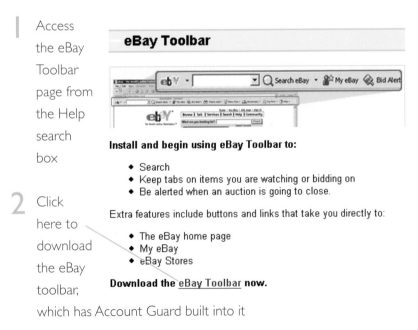

eBay Toolbar

Install and begin using eBay Toolbar to:

- ◆ Search
- ◆ Keep tabs on items you are watching or bidding on
- ◆ Be alerted when an auction is going to close.

Extra features include buttons and links that take you directly to:

- ◆ The eBay home page
- ◆ My eBay
- ◆ eBay Stores

Download the eBay Toolbar now.

2 Click here to download the eBay toolbar, which has Account Guard built into it

3 The presence of Account Guard is denoted by this symbol

Non-payment

One of the unavoidable problems when conducting an auction is non-payment. This occurs when someone places a high bid in an auction, wins the auction and then simply does not pay. The common eBay terminology for this type of behavior is a "deadbeat bidder". The essential thing to remember about non-payment is to make sure you never send any goods until you have received payment. If you are paid by check, make sure the funds have cleared fully before you send the item. If you come across a deadbeat bidder you should try to obtain the funds as follows:

- Contact the buyer directly. Wait a few days and then email with a polite, but firm, request for payment. This should be done at least 3 days after the auction, and within 30 days.

- If there is no response to the initial contact, you can file an Unpaid Item dispute. You have to wait at least 7 days after an auction has closed, and it has to be done within 45 days.

If a user has three Unpaid Item strikes against them they will be barred from eBay.

- Once an Unpaid Item dispute has been filed, eBay contacts the buyer and requests that payment be made, or asks for an explanation about the ongoing non-payment. The buyer then has the chance to pay for the item.

- If the item is still unpaid for, the buyer receives an Unpaid Item strike against their name and you become eligible to relist the item. If this happens, you receive a credit for the Final Value fee from the initial auction and can relist the item for sale without having to pay the listing fee again.

An Unpaid Item dispute can only be open for a total of 60 days.

Second Chance offers

If you have been subjected to a non-paying winning bidder you can offer the item to any of the under-bidders in the auction. This is known as a Second Chance offer. As long as the auction has closed and there is at least one under-bidder then there will be a link to activate this on the auction page and also on the My eBay page. This is a useful way of trying to get some money for the item without having to relist it. However, you will have to accept less than if the high bidder had paid properly. The only fee for a Second Chance offer is the normal Final Value fee.

Inappropriate bidding

The process of bidding in an auction is not exempt from dodges and scams, and there are a number of ways in which users can try to circumvent the normal bidding protocols:

- Unwanted bids. It is perfectly acceptable for a seller to say that they do not want a bid from a particular person. This could be because the bidder has a lot of negative feedback or are bidding from a country to which they are not prepared to send the item. In this case the seller can ask the buyer to withdraw the bid. If this does not work the seller can report them to the eBay investigations team.

If you want to report a user to the eBay Investigations Team, type "investigations" into the search box on the Help section. This contains details of the various types of investigation which can be done by eBay.

- Proxy bidding. This is a tactic where a buyer gets another eBay user to bid on their auction with the intention of pushing up the price. It can be hard to prove, but this type of bidding is not allowed by eBay.

- Shill bidding by the seller. Shill bidding refers to the creation of a secondary User ID, which can then be used by the seller to bid on their own auction, thus pushing up the price in the same way as proxy bidding.

- Shill bidding by the buyer. This occurs when a buyer uses a secondary User ID to place an unrealistically high bid for an item. The intention is that other bidders will see this bid and so be put off the auction. The buyer then uses their other User ID to make a lower bid that becomes the second-highest bid. Then, just before the auction finishes, the initial bid is retracted and the user gets a bargain with their second, lower bid. Although this seems like a good way to win auctions cheaply, it is absolutely against the eBay rules and regulations.

You can legitimately set up more than one User ID. This could be because you want to sell separate types of products and would rather have a different User ID for each one. However, you cannot use these User IDs to bid on your own auctions.

- Vigilante bidding. A lot of eBayers defend its community spirit; this includes trying to sabotage auctions that they see as morally questionable. Targets include ticket sales for large events where someone has bought tickets with a view to making a profit on eBay. Vigilante bidders use additional User IDs to place very high bids for these items, thus scaring off other bidders, and not paying once they win.

No Longer a Registered User

If you break the eBay rules and regulations you could be banned from eBay. If this happens you will be classified as "No Longer a Registered User" (or NARU'd in eBay terminology). If this happens you will not be able to take part in auctions as either a buyer or a seller. Some offences result in instant expulsion, while others operate on a "three strikes and you're out" basis. Some of the offences for which you may be NARU'd on are:

It is possible for users who are NARU'd to re-register under a new User ID. However, when they do this, they will lose any feedback rating that they have built up with their previous User ID.

- Non-payment for items. If you are reported three times for this you will be NARU'd.

- Theft – receiving payment and not sending the goods.

- Account theft, whereby someone steals the account details of another user and pretends to trade as them.

- Selling prohibited items.

Never reveal your User ID or password in reply to an email that has been sent to you. eBay never asks for this type of information in an email; it is a method used by fraudsters to take control of your User ID and your eBay account.

- Trying to sell to a buyer directly by bypassing the auction – contacting them outside the eBay framework and offering to sell them an item that appears in an auction.

- Sending spam emails to eBay members.

- Sending abusive or threatening emails.

- Revealing contact details of eBay members.

- Feedback extortion – threatening to leave negative feedback for another user unless they co-operate with you in some way.

- Providing false information when you register for a User ID. This can include telephone numbers and email addresses.

- Using images from other auction pages.

- Non-payment of eBay fees.

Index

C

D

E

F

G

I

H

J

R

S

T

U